S

Growing From Grief

By Nicola Mansfield

Dedication

I'd like to dedicate this book to my wonderful children, Archie and Ella, and my late husband, John, for being my inspiration. My best friend, Emma, for being my constant source of strength, and my partner, Andy, for always believing in me. I love you all. This book is a tribute to you all.

My entire family and all of my friends and colleagues, you've been a great support. This book wouldn't have been possible without all of you. So, thank you for always being there for me.

About The Author

Nicola Mansfield is a work-from-home Mum raising her beautiful twins, Archie and Ella. She has lived a life that's had its fair share of happiness, love, tragedy, and loss.

She has learnt so much throughout this journey and wants to use the knowledge she has gained to help others and teach herself to be the best version she can be for her children.

Synopsis

I've been told by many people that I have a story that you couldn't make up and needs to be told. After everything that has happened in my life, I feel now is the time to write my story, and by doing this, if I can give even one person hope, then it is worthwhile.

My life has been filled with a lot of happiness, love, tragedy, loss, despair, and hope. Throughout all of this, I have tried to learn from every event that has impacted me, whether it has been good or bad. I hope by reading my book, you will gain something from it. I suppose my main message is never to give up. Life is worth fighting for, no matter what it throws at you. It's how you deal with it that moulds you into the person you were destined to be. I have been lucky enough to have had and still have some incredible people in my life to support and teach me. They pick me up when I fall down and give me the strength to carry on.

Table of Contents

Chapter One - Childhood

As a child, I wasn't one of the popular kids. All I wanted was to be accepted and fit in. I was quiet and a follower. I didn't know who I was or who I wanted to be. Yes, I had friends, but I wasn't the one everyone wanted to have on their team or invited to all the parties. I was just your average 'plain Jane.' I was ok with that.

I had wonderful parents, an older brother Paul, and two dogs. My parents were older than most of my friends' parents. Mum was thirty-five and Dad was forty when I was born. At the time, I didn't realise how lucky I was, but as the years passed, I've certainly learnt that I was exceptionally lucky.

My Dad worked hard to provide for his family and made sure we were healthy, happy, and had lots of holidays. Dad was a self-made man, and he built himself up from nothing. He didn't have the best life growing up, but he certainly made sure he had a future to be proud of, and his children had a better life than he'd had.

My Mum was a stay-at-home Mum looking after my brother and me while my Dad worked. She kept the home clean and tidy, baked, and provided a loving home for her family. She only started working when Paul and I went to school. She wanted to be there for us as much as she could.

Mum was a great cook and always made sure we had home-cooked meals. She'd spend time with us, helping with our homework and teaching us as much as she possibly could. Dad would drive us to our after-school activities. Even after a long day at work, he would always make sure we didn't miss our activities.

As a little girl, I did gymnastics, and every Sunday, Dad would take me to my lessons. He did this for several years before I decided I wanted to follow in my brother's footsteps and learn karate. My parents were happy to support this change in activity, knowing it would provide me with skills to protect myself if I was ever in a bad situation. So twice a week, my Dad would take Paul and I to our lessons, and he would take us to grading's and competitions. My brother was extremely committed to martial arts and, to this day, still does it. I have to say I am exceptionally proud of how well Paul has done. He is well-known in the world of martial arts, travels around the world teaching seminars, and has his own club. I, on the other hand, lost interest, as most teenage girls do. I was more interested in going out with my friends than taking part in karate lessons. Looking back, this was a decision I greatly regret.

We had two beautiful Labradors. Bruce, the eldest, was a black Labrador, and then there was Kim, a chocolate Labrador. She was so cheeky. I remember us losing her as a puppy in the middle of the night, she was eventually found at the bottom of my bed, snuggled up fast asleep and warming my feet. We loved our dogs and took them everywhere we went. I remember coming home from school each day and sitting on the living room floor watching children's TV with her laid on my legs. Kim and I were inseparable. I remember Bruce used to wag his tail all the time. He wagged it so hard that he ended up with a bald patch on it from hitting it against things. Having our dogs was the start of my love of animals. They always brought me so much comfort.

We were very fortunate to grow up in the neighbourhood we lived in, it was a nice area and very safe. Our parents knew when we were out playing in the street, and all the adults kept an eye on all the children. Our street must've had around fifteen children, all around similar ages. This meant when playing out, there was always going to be someone to play with.

We'd spend hours playing so many different games, bulldog, curby, red rover, hide and seek, the list is endless. We all knew when it was time to go in as we'd hear our parents calling us. There was never a dull moment, and we could find ways to entertain ourselves. I had one friend in particular called Tracy, we remained friends throughout our childhood, and even when we went to different comprehensive schools, we still spent time together in the evenings, on weekends, and on holidays.

I remember when I was quite young, Dad was taken into hospital with a blood clot. Mum knew she was able to leave me safely in the care of one of our neighbours while she went with Dad to the hospital. I don't remember a lot about his illness, I just remember it was serious, and I was very lucky it hadn't been worse than it was. I wasn't allowed to go and visit him. I was too young, and Mum and Dad worried it would be too distressing for me to see Dad hooked up to monitors with wires everywhere. I know he was in the hospital for a while, and I missed him so much. Then Dad came home, and I ran into his arms, so happy to have my Dad back home. He sat in his chair, and I leapt onto his knee and cuddled into him. I was not moving off his knee until I had to go to bed. I wanted to make up for all the cuddles I'd missed. He told me how he'd had to walk around with a 'clockwork handbag' that pumped all his medication into him. Even though he was tired, he was being his usual funny self, making light of what had happened and making his little girl laugh. Thankfully Dad fully recovered with no lasting effects from the blood clot.

As a young child, I only ever had one birthday party. It was my seventh birthday, and as my birthday is in the summer, Mum and Dad decided to have a barbeque at home for it. I invited all my friends and had a great afternoon. The one gift that stands out was a Care Bear I received from one of my friends. At this time, Care Bears were really popular, and I really wanted to have one like my friends. I was given a Birthday Bear, and it sat pride of place on the table, leaning against the tomato ketchup bottle. Strange what you remember. My parents were never really fans of parties, but I was so grateful they'd done this for me.

When we were young, Mum and Dad decided if they bought a caravan, we could have regular holidays, including weekends away and longer breaks during the school holidays. I remember Mum picking me up from school and walking to the car park near the school to see Dad sitting in the car with the caravan on the back. The dogs would be in the boot of the car, excited as they knew wherever we were going, there would be new smells and adventures. Paul and I would settle in the backseats playing games on our journey whilst Mum and Dad discussed the route and played music neither of us liked.

We each had responsibilities when we arrived at a campsite. My brother always helped my Dad get the awning up while Mum started organising the inside of the caravan. I was responsible for going to get the water. I felt so grown up having such an important job, and the older I got, the more important jobs I was given. On our holidays, we were a team and worked together to make sure everything was just right so we could start having fun.

We had so many outdoor games that Paul and I would spend hours playing swing ball, badminton, bowls, lawn darts, and whatever else we had for entertainment. If the weather was nice, Mum would be lying on a sun lounger watching us play and finally getting a chance to relax. Dad would potter around getting the barbeque ready for our evening meal or chatting with Mum. As for the dogs, they would be happily lying next to the caravan watching all the comings and goings and wondering where they'd be going for their next walk. In the evenings, we'd have games nights playing Yahtzee or cards. We took a TV with us and watched it occasionally. I remember it having a tiny screen, probably about 10 inches, but it weighed an absolute ton, and Dad would spend ages moving the aerial outside to get a good picture.

We were part of a caravan club which meant we'd get a plaque for each rally we'd attend, there would be activities for us, and there would never be a dull moment. Paul and I were always sporty as children, so we loved the holidays when we would represent our club and compete in various sporting events. We would regularly come home with medals for our achievements. I'll never forget the year we went to a national rally, and I was chosen to raise our club's flag. I was so proud that I'd been picked. As a child, little things pleased you so easily. On the last day of every rally, there would be 'round the flag'. This would be a big meeting where everyone would get together to chat about what they thought of the rally and future events planned for the club and discuss any announcements. In the end, there would always be one adult who had a bucket of sweets for all the kids, sometimes, they would just hand them out, and other times we'd have to chase the adult around the field to get our sweets. I always looked forward to that part of 'round the flag'.

We travelled all over England, and the Lake District was a favourite for all of us. But the holidays that stand out to me were always down south in Cornwall. We'd travel during the night and stop at a service station so Dad could take a break from driving and have a sleep. It was always a big adventure. The holiday that stands out the most was Polzeath. It was fantastic. The site we stayed at was near the beach. I made a friend called Shelly. I can still picture her now with short dark hair and brown eyes. We spent all our holiday together playing games and running around. I remember her Dad used to go shark fishing. I don't know whether he ever caught anything. On this holiday, I remember buying a little dog teddy, and as I didn't know what to call it, I decided to ask my Dad. He was always so good at coming up with names for my stuffed animals. He'd hold them in his hand and really study them before coming out with the perfect name. This time when I asked him what I should call my dog, he responded with the most bizarre name I'd ever heard. "You should call it Eyezirer!" he said. My brother burst into hysterics. I just looked confused. What sort of name was that?! I asked him why and with a very serious expression on his face, he said, "because one eye is higher than the other!". Mum rolled her eyes, and my brother almost wet himself. This was typical Dad, the same man who'd convinced me for years that fairies lived at the bottom of our garden. I only realised he was winding me up when he told me they were called 'fairy enough.' Ever the comedian.

As we got older, we had holidays abroad in the caravan, which I thought was fantastic. By this point, my brother had stopped coming on holiday with us, so it was just my parents and me for these adventures. This didn't stop me from having fun. I remember one year we went to France for three weeks and did a different campsite each week. I loved that the sites had clubhouses and swimming pools and sold amazing cakes! As always, I made friends and was off doing my own thing while my parents relaxed and enjoyed the sunshine. I got to see the amazing sights of France on these holidays, including a trip to Paris. We visited the Eiffel Tower and decided to climb it. Unfortunately, we picked the only leg that didn't have a lift and had to climb the stairs. That was hard work, but it was so worth it to see the amazing view of Paris.

Most of my school friends had holidays abroad in Spain, and even though I was going to all these wonderful places, I still felt like I was missing out. Now that I'm older, I look back on our holidays and realise how great they were. A holiday isn't about exotic places, it's about spending quality time with family and making memories, and we certainly did plenty of that.

I was a normal annoying teenager who thought I knew best and thought it was so unfair when I wasn't allowed the latest things my friends had or wasn't allowed to stay out late like everyone else. I thought it was embarrassing, and my parents didn't understand me, little did I know these were all lessons they were teaching me. I'm sure I caused my parents a lot of heartache over the years. What child doesn't test their parents and push their luck? I was going out in the evening telling my parents I was going to a friend's house when really we were going out buying alcohol, drinking in the park, and smoking cigarettes. Looking back, I realise how stupid I was doing this, especially lying to my parents. We didn't have mobile phones back then, and if something had happened to me, they wouldn't have known anything until they got a knock on the door.

Paul was always the academic one, very intelligent, and did well at school. I, on the other hand, wasn't academic at all. At times I felt like a disappointment to my parents, not that they made me feel that I was. My Mum once told me, "Your brother may be intelligent, but you go out and make things happen. If you want something, you go and get it". This has stuck with me ever since, and when I feel I'm not doing well, I remember my Mum's reassuring words.

Paul was very focused. He knew what he wanted to do. I, on the other hand, didn't have a clue what I wanted to do. I left school with one GCSE in Art, which was not what I was hoping for, considering how hard I had studied for my exams. So I went to college straight from school. I studied Beauty Therapy for a year and then decided I didn't like it. Then went on to do Art and Design for three years. I don't know why, as I never managed to get employment in the design industry. I ended up taking the first job I could get in a call centre as an operator, which I thought would tie me over until I worked out what I wanted to do. I was very fortunate while I was there as I was able to work my way up the company, eventually becoming a Call Centre Manager. I was eventually made redundant after working there for ten years and decided to look for a career change. I then landed a great new role as a Tutor working within the Welfare to Work industry. I loved this. I was helping unemployed people get their lives back by helping them improve their skills and gain employment. I again was lucky enough to land a Performance Manager role and ran one of the offices in the area. When the contract came to an end, I was sad to be leaving my team, but it was time for new pastures. I went back to being a Tutor for a while before landing a Tutor role within the local college, teaching apprentices to work for the call centre I used to work for. It was meant to be, I loved this role and did it for many months before circumstances changed, and I had to stop working.

My Mum and Dad worked hard to raise us with strong values, I can't speak on behalf of my brother about what he has learnt, but I can certainly say they taught us well. Dad taught me that it doesn't matter where you come from. If you work hard, you can achieve anything you put your mind to. He started at the bottom and worked his way up, having a very successful career. Mum was fortunate to have had a better childhood and worked hard to become a strong independent woman. Mum taught me about strength, resilience, determination, and never giving up, no matter how hard the fight is. She encouraged me to follow my dreams.

As parents, all they ever wanted was for us to be happy and healthy, settle down with loving partners, and have our own families. They didn't hand everything to us on a plate. They taught us we had to work hard for things. Even as children, this was a lesson they made sure we knew. If we worked hard, we would be rewarded. As a child, I just thought they were tougher than other parents because they were older. I didn't realise being older meant they'd had more life experience and were passing on the lessons they hadn't along the way. Looking back, I am so thankful our parents took the time to teach us so much, whilst giving us a stable, loving home to grow up in.

When Paul was older, he went off to university and eventually flew the nest in pursuit of his dreams. After spending time in various countries, he eventually settled in America, where he now lives and has two amazing children. He works extremely hard to be a good father, and I know my parents would be proud of him. I, on the other hand, was always a home bird, and although I wanted to travel, I couldn't stand the thought of leaving my parents. So I stayed at home and built my life near them, not realising one day I would find out why it was so important that I stayed.

Chapter Two - Mum

When I was seventeen, we found out Mum was ill. She was diagnosed with Multiple Myeloma, a form of blood cancer. She'd been feeling unwell for a while but kept it from us. It was only after numerous visits to the doctors she found out the cause. The day she sat us down and told us she had cancer, I thought my world had fallen apart. How could my Mum have cancer? She doesn't drink, smoke, or take drugs and looks after herself. How can this happen? One of the first questions she asked the doctor was, “is this hereditary?” She was a typical Mum thinking of us before herself. No was the answer. She was started on a course of chemotherapy. The specialist advised this would get cancer under control. She had to have a minor operation so they could fit a Hickman line into her chest for her treatment. Mum was so brave she even watched the procedure. I asked her why she watched them she said, “it’s my body, and I want to know what they’re doing to it.” Another thing that stuck with me over the years.

Her first treatment was successful, and she went into remission. We were over the moon, so Mum carried on with life as normal. By this point, her father had been ill for a while. We’d visited regularly and never knew on each visit if it would be the last one.

I shared a special bond with my Grandpa. We would sit for hours playing games together but never talking, and yet somehow, we always knew what each other was thinking. I idolised him. He would take me to the bowling club and fall asleep with me sitting on his knee, cuddling into him. I remember he always smelled of stale tobacco. I didn't care because that was his smell, so when he finally passed, it hit me hard. Life without my Grandpa was a scary thought. This was my first experience with death, and it scared me. Although I was a teenager, by the time he passed, I still didn't understand fully.

At this point, I was starting with depression but didn't realise it. It took one of our dogs dying for me to hit rock bottom. With Mum's cancer, Grandpa dying then my dog I had grown up with dying, I felt if this is what life is about, I don't want to be part of it. That night I found a bottle of paracetamol in the bathroom and decided to take all 26 tablets. How I was only sick is beyond me. Mum and Dad had no idea what I'd done or why I was sick. I never told them what I did. At first, I was annoyed that I hadn't died, but then I realised I couldn't die, yet my family needed me. Mum knew something wasn't right with me, so she took me to the doctor, who told her I was depressed. Mum couldn't understand how I could be depressed at seventeen but agreed that counselling might help. I was also put on Prozac. I soon started picking back up and was more like myself again.

Unfortunately, Mum's remission only lasted a few years, and cancer came back. This time she needed a stronger course of chemotherapy, which would result in her losing her hair. Mum didn't take this well. I told her I'd go with her to her appointment to be fitted with a wig and would be there every step of the way. She got her wig before it was needed but was reassured that when the time came, at least it was there. When her hair started falling out, Mum was very emotional. Finding bits of hair on her pillow must've been hard. She couldn't brush her hair without bits coming out. At this point, she wanted her hair cut but couldn't face going to a hairdresser, so I stepped in and cut it for her. I didn't let her see how upsetting this was. I knew this wasn't about me. It was about her, and she needed me to be strong. After this, I would regularly give her pamper sessions, giving her facials and manicures so that she'd feel better about herself and I'd get to spend time with her.

During Mum's illness, she also developed kidney failure and therefore needed to go on dialysis. Yet another blow for Mum but her strength and determination shone through. She was determined to beat cancer and kidney failure. We asked if a kidney replacement would work, but unfortunately, cancer would cause the kidney to fail again. This didn't deter Mum's fighting spirit. She spent a lot of time in and out of the hospital and then started dialysis at home. Dad converted my old bedroom into a quiet room where she could have her treatment without interruption and relax.

Time went by, and Mum was doing well until cancer came back again. She'd coped with the sickness, and the hair loss before, so she was ready again, but this time it hit her harder. With kidney failure as well, it was a tougher fight for her this time round, her skin was sore, and she was even more tired than before, but yet again, it didn't deter her fighting spirit. She then developed peritonitis, and this drained her. She was so ill and spent a few weeks in the hospital having treatment and getting her strength back. I remember going to see her one day, and she told me how dry her skin was. I sat on her bed, massaging cream into her legs and arms. She smiled at me and said, "You shouldn't have to do this," I told her, "She'd looked after me all my life. It was my turn to look after her". She told me how proud she was of me and that she wished I didn't have to see her like this. Inside, my heart was breaking. I smiled at her and said, "No matter what, I will be here for you right till the end, holding your hand. The last words you'll hear from me will be, Mum, I love you." We both cried and hugged each other. I knew I was going to lose her. I just didn't know when.

Paul and his wife at the time came to visit with their daughter a few months later. Mum got to meet her first grandchild and was so happy. She appeared strong and vibrant again and enjoyed every minute of their visit. After they left, I was due to go on holiday to Mexico. She made me promise not to call while I was away as I knew she'd be going into the hospital for treatment and that she'd be fine. I wasn't even allowed to call on my birthday. I'd never had a birthday where I hadn't at least spoken to her, but I promised her I wouldn't, so off I went.

Partway through my holiday, I felt something wasn't right. Every time I thought of Mum, I'd get upset. The closer it got to my birthday, the stronger the feeling was. I put it down to missing and worrying about her and was due home a few days later.

Unfortunately, my instincts were right. Something was wrong, and I arrived home full of life after enjoying an amazing holiday and so many new experiences. Shortly after I returned home, there was a knock at my door. I opened it to see Paul and my Dad standing there. At first, I was overjoyed to see them both until reality hit, and I realised my brother should have been at his home in America. They took me into the house and sat me down. Dad couldn't speak. Paul explained to me that Mum had been in hospital as she wasn't feeling well. She passed away the day after my birthday, four hours after my birthday, to be precise. I felt my world come crashing down around me. My heart was breaking. I had lost my Mum and never had the chance to say goodbye. I questioned myself so many times. "What were the last words I said to her? Did I tell her I loved her?." I had promised my Mum when the time came, I would be by her side, and the last words she'd hear were, "Mum, I love you." I felt I'd broken a promise to her and hated the fact I'd been enjoying myself on holiday.

As time went by, I started to understand that this was what she had wanted. She didn't want me to watch her die. She wanted me to go and enjoy life. Paul and I believe she waited to meet her first grandchild and for me to go away, she knew her time was coming and held on as long as she could. I was told that before she passed, she knew she was going to die and that she was scared. My Dad had received the call telling him she was getting worse during the night, and he couldn't bring himself to go to her. For a while, I was angry that he didn't go to her and hold her hand so she wasn't alone. I hated the thought of strangers being the last faces she saw instead of her family. Dad told me if I'd been there, he would've gone again. This caused me so much anger, but in time I realised there was a reason for this my Dad wasn't well himself.

Mum's funeral was extremely hard and emotional. Although I'd been to the funeral of my Grandparents, I wasn't prepared for this. Paul and I chose two of Mum's favourite songs, "My heart will go on" by Celine Dion and "Time to say goodbye" by Sarah Brightman and Andrea Bochelli. Both songs still bring me to tears. They were so appropriate for her funeral. It was nice to see how many people came to pay their respects, from neighbours in their street to members of their Golf Club. It was clear to see how loved, and respected Mum was.

I was twenty-four when I lost Mum, I'd barely started my life, and now I was faced with a future without the one person I turned to whenever I needed guidance and reassurance.

My Mum will always be my inspiration and hero. When you lose someone so dear, it really shows you that you lost so much more than you ever realised and that you need to appreciate everyone around you.

I struggle with the fact that Mum never got to see me happy or see me get married. She never got to meet my husband or her grandchildren. She would've been a fantastic Gran and a huge part of their lives. I make sure every day her memory lives on.

Chapter Three - Dad

Throughout the last few years of Mum's illness, it became apparent that something wasn't right with my Dad. He was getting forgetful and also fainting a lot. He was referred to a specialist, and tests began. He was diagnosed with an irregular heartbeat and needed surgery to have a pacemaker fitted. It was a straightforward procedure, and Dad stopped passing out. However, his memory continued to be a problem. He went through further testing, and still no diagnosis. It wasn't until several years after my Mum passed away that we finally got answers.

Dad was diagnosed with Alzheimer's and Vascular Dementia. I'd already taken over dealing with all the household things after losing Mum, as he said he couldn't deal with them. At the time, I thought this was laziness, but I realised after his diagnosis that he probably asked me to deal with it all as he didn't know how to.

I managed to keep Dad at home for eight years with help from neighbours who would check on him whilst I was at work. As time went on, he needed more and more help at home. He needed help with preparing meals and his personal hygiene and, eventually, wasn't safe to go out on his own.

I found these eight years extremely difficult. One day I found myself driving in my car and thought, 'Would it matter if I drove into a brick wall' I knew this wasn't a good sign, but after feeling suicidal as a teenager, I recognised the signs this time and called my doctor. I knew I needed help. It turned out to be the best thing I could've done as I was having a nervous breakdown. I was referred to a counsellor, and after numerous sessions, I was finally back in a place where I felt strong again. I had to be strong. My Dad needed me.

I remember one day, I received a call from his neighbour telling me he'd gone out several hours earlier and still hadn't returned home. After panicking and searching for him, eventually, he came home without a care in the world. He'd had a lovely trip to Whitby. Shortly after that, I had to make the decision to have his driving licence taken away. It was clear he was becoming a danger on the road. I felt awful completing the form and explained to him due to his illness, this was a procedure and that it may result in his licence being revoked. He loved driving as it gave him freedom, and he knew taking it away would mean he'd get worse, but I had to reason which was worse, him killing someone or his illness getting worse. Obviously, the safety of himself and other people had to come first.

As you can guess, yes, he did get worse quickly. Without his freedom, he became a prisoner in his own home, so day-care began. He went to a local care home that specialised in Alzheimer's patients and enjoyed day-care. He was safe, fed, cared for, and had company. He still had support from his neighbour, who would take him and collect him and help him with his personal care. We were both very lucky to get this much support from his neighbour. This enabled me to carry on working full time, and Dad didn't feel like he was a burden on me. I helped out whenever I could and visited Dad most days. He wanted me to focus on my own life and enjoy myself.

Dad would have respite care at the care home every now and then to give his neighbour and me a break. One day I went to pick him up, and he refused to come home, "This is my home," he told me, I asked if he could stay another day, and I'd try to take him home the next day. Dad never did come home. He refused to leave, and part of me was relieved that he'd made the decision for himself, as I was dreading the day of telling him he had to go into full-time care. He'd always told my brother and me as kids, "If I ever need to go into a care home, shoot me!". I knew by this point he'd lost a lot of who he was. My father was slowly slipping away from me. We hadn't had a great relationship when I was a child, yes, he'd always been there for me and provided for me, but we were never close. All that changed when we lost Mum. Our relationship went from strength to strength. We needed each other. So to see my Dad change from the intelligent, independent, strong man he'd been to the man he was becoming was heart-breaking.

As the years passed, he was happy in the care home, he loved the staff, and the staff loved him. He remained the polite man he'd always been and was enjoying his own company but also sitting with other residents during the day. Year by year, more and more of Dad faded away. When the time came that he didn't know who I was, I was devastated. "Why doesn't he know me? I'm his daughter. How can he forget me?", questions I'd ask myself over and over. Gradually Dad lost his independence and his dignity.

Eventually, he became a little old man I'd go to see, he thought I was a friend, so I'd humour him. I'd tell him I was his daughter but stopped getting upset that he didn't know me. It wasn't his fault his memory had been taken away from him. He didn't remember anything or anyone from his life, so what was inside his head? Your guess is as good as mine. No idea. He was happy, healthy, and well cared for, so I couldn't ask for anything else.

He would often come out with some hilarious stories. One time, he told me Michael Jackson was his friend. Michael had apparently taken Dad's watch away to get fixed. He thought this was fantastic. Other times he'd keep asking me over and over when I was going. I never knew from one visit to the next what he'd come out with. He was always happy and full of smiles even though he didn't know who I was.

Paul visited numerous times over the years, and with every visit, he thought it would be the last time he'd see Dad. He said his goodbyes and prepared himself. Yet Dad kept going, surprising us all with his strength. Watching someone you love to lose everything that made them who they are is heart-breaking. You see them gradually forget every aspect of their life, and everyone they love becomes a distant memory that eventually disappears. Just their body is left. Their spirit left years ago. I knew this every time I looked at Dad. I grieved for the loss of my father, the hugs only a Dad can give his little girl, and our conversations where he'd have me laughing about stories from his past. Every time I received a call from the care home telling me Dad wasn't well, I feared I was going to lose him. This carried on for seven years until, one day, that call came.

Dad was struggling to breath, the doctor was with him, and I had to get there fast. Walking in and seeing this frail little old man struggling to breath hit me hard, and the tears fell. Without the doctors or nurses saying, I knew it was time. My best friend came to the care home for support and stayed with me until late in the evening. I held Dad's hand and told him it was time to let go, and it was ok, Mum would be waiting for him. He was unconscious, but I knew he could hear me. He carried on breathing for a short while. After that, he finally took his last breath. I felt my heart break again. I'd lost another parent. I was conflicted with emotions, devastated my Dad was gone but also relieved as he was no longer suffering. He was with Mum again.

Paul flew home, and together we arranged his funeral. We spent the week talking about our childhood, our parents, and how they helped us become the people we are today. Even though we had no parents to turn to now, we knew we were so lucky we had had our Mum and Dad. Thankfully my brother and I have a great relationship and are very close even though we live on opposite sides of the world to each other. No matter what, we will always have each other.

Dad's funeral was very small. He had lost touch with people since Mum had passed away. It ended up being a handful of people, including friends and neighbours. We picked two songs for Dad's funeral, 'Bridge over troubled water' by Simon and Garfunkel, a favourite of Dad's, and 'The Prayer' by

Celine Dion and Andrea Bochelli. The words felt as though it was Paul and I singing it to him.

Alzheimer's and Dementia are cruel diseases that rob people of their very essence. They may not suffer from pain, but they suffer in ways you wouldn't let an animal suffer. It destroys your independence, your dignity, and your mind. Hopefully, one day a cure will be found. In the meantime, families will be put through heartache watching their loved ones disappear.

Chapter Four - Friendship

As you know, I never had lots of friends, but the friends I do have are quality friends. I have two friendships that have stood the test of time and mean the world to me.

My first is Ann-Marie, we have been friends for twenty-seven years. I met Ann-Marie when I was seventeen. I worked in the local Newsagents with her Mum. She used to come in to see her Mum, and we'd always end up chatting.

After a while, we decided to go swimming one evening. I can't even remember why we chose swimming, but I'm glad we did. We only ever went once. After that, our weekly outing would be to the pub instead. This was a much more enjoyable night for us. Gradually our nights out became more frequent, and other friends started joining in. We would go to karaoke nights and various pubs three or four nights a week. We had a fantastic group of friends and always had a great time. Considering the amount of alcohol we used to drink, I'm surprised we were capable of going out as often as we did.

I had my first grown-up holiday with Ann-Marie. I was in my late teens and getting to have my first-ever holiday with my friends, and I was beyond excited. We decided to go to Turkey, and three of us went. Me Ann-Marie, and our friend

Alison, it was always the three of us everywhere we went. We went for a week with plenty of sunshine, copious amounts of drinking alcohol, and loads of fun. We made a couple of day trips and a bit of shopping, but we're more interested in lounging by the pool all day and then partying the night away and drinking cocktails. Ann-Marie and Alison opened my eyes to the world of freedom away from the rules of being at home. I was starting to learn about being an adult, ok it was only the fun side I was experiencing, but I was living my life and loving it. It will always be a holiday I remember fondly.

As you get older, friendships change as you meet your partners, settle down and start a family. I was so happy for Ann-Marie when she met her husband and started a family. We still kept in contact and saw each other when we could. This friendship has continued over the years, and Ann-Marie has been there for me through so many challenging times. Even if we go weeks without catching up, I know she is always at the end of the phone if I ever need her.

My second is Emma. I met Emma when we both worked in a call centre. Emma joined my team when she was pregnant with her first child. We became solid friends. As time went on, I became Auntie to her children, and she would become Auntie to mine.

We have had many drunken nights out enjoying ourselves over the years. And also had nights of chilling out, watching DVDs, and chatting about everything and nothing. We have been there for each other through thick and thin. We have developed the kind of friendship that is more than that. Emma knows me better than anyone in the world. She is the one person I trust completely. She sees my flaws and my barriers and still loves me for me, and encourages me to be true to myself. She's the kind of friend I needed to bring me out of my shell and help me learn about who I was really supposed to be.

Emma has been by my side through the darkest of days and the most magical times of my life. How can you truly express what a friend like this really means? All I can say is, without her, my life would be very different.

Chapter Five - John

I was thirty by the time I found John, the man who became my future. I had a couple of long-term relationships, some of which I thought would go somewhere but never did. As time went on, I was convinced I would never meet the one, my biological clock was ticking, and I felt that time was running out for me to settle down and start a family. I gave up on looking and just accepted that there were no decent men out there that wanted me. A friend at work was sick of me moping around and thinking like this and decided to try and set me up with his partner's son John. I thought, why not? What have I got to lose?

We started talking on Facebook, to begin with, and shortly after that, we had our first date in August of 2008. It wasn't your usual kind of first date. We'd decided to have it at my house with a takeaway and a film. To this day, I can't tell you about the film we watched or the title, and we spent the whole time talking about anything and everything. When we shared our first kiss, it felt like a movie moment to me. If I'd been standing up, I would've kicked my leg out behind me. I felt sparks and flutters, and at that moment, I knew I was going to spend the rest of my life with John. Obviously, I didn't tell him this for fear of him running a mile.

As time went on, we spent more and more time together, and when we weren't together, we were constantly texting or calling each other. It felt so right. John was everything I'd wanted. He was kind, and caring, made me laugh, and had a fantastic sense of humour. He didn't take life too seriously and wanted to live each day for the moment. On the plus side, he was extremely handsome with dimples. I'd always loved dimples. He had a way of making me feel like I was the only person in the room, every time I saw him, I got butterflies in my stomach. I was falling for him fast.

Within a few months, John moved in with me only because the place he was living in would no longer be available to him. John had the option of either going back to his Dad's house or moving in with me. As he was spending most of his time at my house, we thought, why not? The decision was made. We'd go out whenever we wanted to, spend time with friends, and were so happy. John confessed after several months that he, too, had felt a spark when we first kissed and had thought the same as me. He knew I was going to become his wife.

John proposed in July 2009. He'd planned a dinner with some friends and family and even organised a cake with 'Will you marry me' on it. I know his proposal was beautiful. However, I can't remember exactly what he said. He told me it felt like hours from him asking me to me saying 'yes.' I kept looking at him, the cake, and the ring, and eventually said 'yes.' I was ecstatic. I'd found my soulmate and was going to be his wife. How perfect our life would become. We had talked about what we both wanted for our future, so I knew we were on the same page. The next year was spent planning our wedding and decorating our home as we were moving into Dad's house as he'd gone into full-time care.

We didn't want a huge wedding and knew we couldn't afford one, so we kept it very intimate. On June 11th, 2010, we got married at the registry office, I walked down the aisle to 'Greatest Day' by Take That, and we walked out as husband and wife to 'I belong to you' by Anastasia. The songs were perfect and reflected our thoughts exactly. The ceremony was very emotional for us both, with a small gathering of family and friends there. When it came to exchanging rings, we had a giggle as John's ring would not go on his finger. I'd joked, 'You're the wrong one,' and he laughed, and magically the ring suddenly went on. We had our wedding photos taken at a local park with some beautiful scenery and then returned to our home for the reception. We'd had a marquee put in the back garden. The buffet was done by a family friend. We provided a free bar and made a playlist on the laptop, and connected it to some speakers. It was hard that my Mum wasn't here to see me get married, and Dad was in no fit state by this point to attend our wedding. However, my brother flew halfway around the world to be there. He only got to meet John a few days before our wedding. Luckily they connected instantly and began their brotherly bond. They'd spend hours talking about Karate as, by this point, Paul was running his own club in America. John was in awe of him and was so happy they had so much in common. I remember finding them later in the evening, away from all our guests chatting away while having a drink. I knew at that point I was so lucky John had picked me and was over the moon that my brother loved him too.

Our first dance was to 'Hold On' by Michael Buble. The words were perfect. Throughout our marriage, that song gave us strength and took on new meaning in every event. As we danced, John felt embarrassed as all eyes were on us and joked about the length of the song. I didn't care. I was in my husband's arms, the happiest woman alive, and that's where I planned to stay.

The next year was happy married life. We were saving up for our honeymoon, so we tightened our belts to ensure we had the holiday of a lifetime. In June 2011, we flew out to California to stay with Paul and his family. My brother's children took to John immediately. He was like a child himself most of the time, so he was happy to play for hours with them. They'd play in the swimming pool, run around like lunatics, and climb all over him. He was in his element. I got a glimpse of the type of father he would be and loved what I saw. During our trip, Paul had planned an amazing road trip for us all. We set off to the Grand Canyon, which was incredible. John was so relaxed and amazed by the beauty of the place.

We got some great photos of John and Paul in various fighting poses with the canyon in the background. We then went on to National Zion Park, another amazing and beautiful place, stopping at Utah before heading to Las Vegas. What a contrast from all the nature and beauty to a place as vibrant as Vegas. We were certainly getting the full experience. Paul had kindly booked us a beautiful suite in the MGM grand hotel. We were blown away. It was huge. We were reluctant to leave it for a couple of reasons. We strolled along the strip, hung out by the pool, and saw a couple of shows in between luxury buffets and drinking sessions. It was incredible. I remember in one of the restaurants, John ordered a cheeseburger, he said it was the most amazing cheeseburger he'd ever eaten and how it melted in his mouth. He loved being in America. After a few days in Vegas, we were exhausted and ready for a few relaxing days by the pool back home before jumping on an airplane to head back to the UK and reality. No amount of words could ever let Paul and his family know how grateful we both were for our trip. It was an absolute dream, a trip we would never forget.

On the way home, we talked about the possibility of moving to America and starting a new life. The opportunities for us there would be endless, it gave us something to think about. The life our children could have and the education they'd receive would be amazing. Imagine raising our family over there, and we'd have family close by supporting us. Paul had always wanted me to move to America, and now it looked like it could be a possibility. I knew he'd help us get set up with a house and help us find jobs. This was something we needed to think long and hard about. Leaving our friends and family behind would be hard, but we had to think about our future together.

We got back home and settled back into normal life. We were both exhausted from our trip. However, John was taking longer to recover from his jet lag. Two weeks later, on July 20th, 2011, John collapsed at work with a seizure. He was rushed to hospital. There he had a further two seizures. By the time I got there, he was barely conscious and looked dreadful. He had burst blood vessels all over his face, and he looked like he was wearing a mask as it was across his eyes and cheeks. There was no explanation for why this had happened. He was taken up to ICU, where he spent his first night barely conscious. Family and friends had come to the hospital. No one knew what to do. All we knew was that something was really wrong, and we had no idea what. I stayed with John all night by his bed, barely sleeping and watching him breath waiting for him to come round properly. A specialist came to see him the next day and did a lumbar puncture. They suspected he had some kind of infection. According to the specialist, John was lucky to have survived the seizures; they were so severe. It didn't make sense. John was the picture of health, and he looked after his body as though it was a temple.

Once he regained consciousness, he was moved onto a ward and given medication to fight whatever infection he may have had. It was his birthday on the 23rd, so several friends and family came to visit, making a big fuss about him. I found out later he didn't remember his birthday or mine, which was two days later. All I cared about was getting him well and back home where he belonged. After a week in the hospital, he was transferred to another one with a neurology ward, where he spent a further two weeks regaining his strength. He had a head scan and various tests, and eventually, they decided he had viral encephalitis, a virus that attacks the brain tissue. We still didn't know why it had happened, but at least he seemed to be getting better. He was given medication to stop the seizures and went from strength to strength. His memory had been affected slightly, but they thought that he would return to normal once he returned to normal life again.

It was August now, and John had returned home, and we got on with life again. He was due another brain scan and a follow-up appointment in September with the specialist to ensure he was doing ok. In early September, we were told that the scan hadn't improved and that the specialist suspected John had a brain tumour and was now being referred to a neurosurgeon to find out more. We were in absolute shock but thought we didn't know all the facts yet. Let's wait and see what the neurosurgeon has to say. We met with the neurosurgeon on September 12th, 2011, where we were told John had a grade 2 brain tumour that he'd probably had all of his life. As it was grade two, this meant it was low-level and would be monitored before any course of action would be decided. He had an MRI scan, a Thalion scan, and a CT scan, and his neurosurgeon was happy there hadn't been any changes. He had three months before his next check-up, so again John resumed normal life working, going to Karate, and enjoying life.

On December 10th, John became ill again, this time throwing up. He'd had headaches for several days, so I called the doctor, and he was admitted to the hospital again. He spent four days there having scans done and being treated before he returned home. I received a call from his neurosurgeon on the 21st of December asking me to bring John in the following day. I knew something was wrong, but John kept telling me to stop worrying. The following day we attended his appointment and were told the tumour had grown, and due to the speed of the growth, we couldn't afford to take action. He needed surgery to remove the tumour and have a biopsy. This was planned for the new year. John handled the news extremely well, telling me everything would be fine. I, on the other hand, was falling apart inside. I was terrified I would lose him, but I tried to stay strong for him.

On January 2nd, 2012, I took John to the hospital to be admitted for surgery the following day. I hated leaving him that night but knew I could return the following morning to sit with him until he went down to the theatre at 12:30 pm. I barely slept that night. John, on the other hand, had slept well and was his usual happy-go-lucky self. I went down to the theatre with him and was able to say goodbye. I was crying by this point. John had tears in his eyes. He told me he loved me and not to worry as he'd see me soon. Throughout the afternoon, I was a nervous wreck and couldn't stop thinking about the surgery and whether he was ok. I drove back to the hospital at 6 pm and waited. He eventually came out of surgery at 6:50 pm and was in recovery. I didn't get to see him until 8 pm when he was brought back to the ward and put in the high-dependency unit. I was so surprised by how well he looked, even though he had plastered all over and a tube coming out of his head to drain away any excess blood. His right eye was closed and swollen, and an oxygen mask, a drip going into him, and a catheter, yet he was doing well and cracking jokes. I was so relieved. My beloved husband was going to be ok.

He stayed in the high-dependency unit for a couple of days as they were concerned about his speech, but this gradually improved. I was told most of his tumour had been removed and sent off for a biopsy. The results would take a week. I bumped into his neurosurgeon in the corridor a couple of days later and thanked him. He sat me down and asked how I was doing and explained that he was pleased with how the surgery went and that there were only a few fibres remaining that he was unable to remove. He had a feeling, based on what he'd seen, John would need treatment but would know more once the results were back. To my amazement, John was sent home a few days later and told to rest.

We returned to see his neurosurgeon on the 12th of January. He was pleased with how John was recovering and went on to explain the results. John's tumour had gone from a grade two to a grade four, the highest level, and it was malignant. The type of tumour was called an astrocytoma. I started crying. John said, "It's ok. What happens now?" Given John's age and health, his neurosurgeon was keen to start treatment which would start in six weeks. He arranged another appointment for the following week to meet the oncologist to discuss radiotherapy and chemotherapy. We were given booklets to read to help us get our heads round this. When we got in the car, I broke down, I had a feeling the news wouldn't be good, but I wasn't prepared for this. How could my John have cancer? It didn't make any sense. As always, John was strong and focused on all the positives and told me not to worry. He wasn't going anywhere.

The next few days were extremely difficult. I had to tell all of John's family what had been said, along with my brother and our friends. It was easier for John if I told them as I could explain it. Although his speech and memory hadn't been affected, he still found it difficult to explain things. Throughout this time, I would go from being strong to crying, constantly wanting answers I knew we'd never get. We were worried the treatment would affect John's fertility as we really wanted to start a family, so we knew this was a question we needed to ask the oncologist.

Whilst waiting for the oncology appointment, we talked a lot about our thoughts and fears. John remained focused that he was going to beat it. He knew there was a chance of remission and it coming back, but his goal was to annihilate it permanently. His attitude reminded me a lot of Mum, his strength and determination to fight this. I wished he'd had the chance to meet her. I think they would've got on really well. I was inspired by him and admired the way he handled everything. It made me love him even more if that was possible.

On the 18th of January, we met with John's neurosurgeon and oncologist to discuss his treatment. He would be undergoing radiotherapy once a mask was made for a few minutes five times a week for six weeks. The treatment would make him feel sick and very tired for the first three weeks, but it would be worth it. He would also have chemotherapy tablets five days a week for six months. With the aim that by the end of the course, he would not require any further treatment for a long time, if ever. His blood count would be monitored closely, and he would be more at risk of infections and viruses and may require a blood transfusion, but this was all ifs and buts. Three months after treatment, he'd have another scan to see how he was progressing. Although they didn't feel his fertility would be affected by the treatment, they also thought it might be wise to freeze his sperm just in case. That was arranged and put to the back of our minds.

We'd actually planned on trying for a family in 2012 but decided, given everything that was happening to John, we needed to put all our energy and focus into getting him through his treatment and healthy. We had plenty of time to start a family once he was better.

During the last few weeks, I had taken time off work to be there every step of the way with John and help him regain his strength after his surgery. I was dreading going back to work and leaving him, but we needed the money. Me staying at home wasn't an option. My work was so supportive, helping me phase back into my duties. I didn't have the confidence I'd had before, so I struggled to deal with groups of people. I had a lot of pent-up anger and would get easily wound up at little things. Luckily,

I got to work with my colleagues, supporting them rather than being out on my own like I normally would be.

John and I continued talking about everything whilst waiting for his treatment. He hid a lot of his own worries as he was so concerned about me. From some of the questions he'd ask, I wondered how much he actually understood about what could happen. He told me one day that he didn't want to die as he didn't want to leave me. We had to focus on him beating this. We'd waited long enough to find each other, and we weren't going to be robbed of our happily ever after.

On February 14th, John started his treatment. We had several appointments running up to this day to prepare John. Blood tests, discussions about what to expect and what possible side effects, who would see him on each appointment, and how often checks would be done. The oncology unit was great, and they were so friendly, supportive, and very thorough with their information. We were ready to face this, so the battle commenced - trips to the hospital five times a week. As I was back at work, John's Dad would take him and sit with him after his appointments until I got home. This was extremely frustrating for me. I felt my place was by John's side but knew that wasn't possible. John understood and looked forward to me coming home to him every night. After the first week, John was doing well. No side effects had started. His first course of treatment finally finished on the 26th of March, and we knew he'd carry on with his chemotherapy, the hardest part was over. John had coped exceptionally well throughout. Even though he had tiredness, nausea, and hair loss, he took it all in his stride.

The next few months consisted of trying to get on with our lives. John had his second round of chemotherapy and various appointments to monitor him. He had an eye appointment that we hoped would give us some hope for his eye-opening again. However, that wasn't the case. Due to the position of John's tumour, his eyes had been damaged, his left eye remained closed, and he had lost 60% of the peripheral vision in his right eye. He would now be registered as partially sighted and had to learn how to adjust. Once his treatment was finished, there was a chance he could go to a rehabilitation unit to help him regain control of his life and rebuild his strength. John struggled with this news as we'd thought he would return to how he used to be. We both felt angry, like we'd been given false hope. By this stage, due to all the medication he had been on, he had developed 'moon face syndrome', causing his face to swell. John told me he didn't think he was good enough for me anymore and that I needed someone better. I was shocked by his words. I made it clear that there was nobody better than him, and regardless of how he looked or what he could and couldn't do, he was my husband, and I loved him just as much, if not more, than the day I married him. Both our emotions were up and down as it grew nearer the date of John's next scan. We were anxious and praying this scan would show that all the treatment had worked and we could start looking to the future again.

On the 27th of June, we went to see John's neurosurgeon to get his MRI scan results. This was the day our future was destroyed. John's tumour had come back and was bigger than before. It was spreading through his brain. No amount of treatment was going to save him now. No one knew how long he had and would knowing actually make a difference. We just knew John was given a death sentence, a young man with his whole life ahead of him for no good reason, and his life was being cut short. Due to the tumour, John's reaction was completely unexpected. He laughed and was not bothered in the slightest. His oncologist said it was a blessing he was placid, as the opposite would have been even more painful. John was eventually going to need round-the-clock care. He would lose the ability to care for himself and lose his eyesight and his speech. I couldn't get my head around it. How would I cope without John? He was my reason for living, my whole world. I was devastated. We'd only just had our second wedding anniversary. Would he even get to meet his children? We hadn't had enough time together. John held me most of that day and told me that no matter what, he would always be with me. I realised that night I had to make every second of every day count for John. He needed to see how much I loved him and bring him as much happiness as possible. Family and friends rallied round, supporting us both in any way they could. I was able to spend time with John, work, and do all my necessary jobs whilst John rested and spent time with all the people who loved him.

I hated having to sort out Solicitor's appointments, so John's affairs were all in order, it felt so wrong, but I didn't have a choice. We knew we both wanted John to stay at home; it was where he belonged, so district nurses, occupational health, and Macmillan nurses all did their part in ensuring our home was safe, and everything was in place that needed to be.

John's character started to come back. He was laughing and joking with everyone. We said he'd lost his filter as he would say things that you really shouldn't say out loud. We'd always laugh at how inappropriate some of his comments would be, but we knew he couldn't help it, so we made sure we kept giving him a reason to smile. It was as though he had made peace with his fate and was determined to make the most of every day he had left. This made me love and admire him even more. I was so proud to be his wife.

In August, thanks to the Willow Foundation, we started planning our last holiday together. We spent three wonderful days in a beautiful hotel in Windermere in the Lake District. John coped amazingly well. We'd go for short walks in the sunshine and sit and talk for hours. He slept when he got tired, and I stayed by his side. We talked about what our children would be like and picked their names. Archie John for our son, Archie, was chosen as we'd made friends with a cheeky black Labrador during our trip. We thought our son would need a name with a character. Ella Kate for our daughter, there had been a singer on the X Factor we'd liked the previous year and thought her name would be perfect. We talked as though our future would be together and spent our days in a magical bubble ignoring the reality of what was going to happen in the next few months. By the time we returned home, we were both feeling uplifted and grateful for the time we'd spent away. John was exhausted, so he spent most of his time sleeping over the next few days. It was understandable he had really pushed himself.

After our holiday, I thought long and hard about our dream of becoming parents and what it would mean to John if he knew he was a Dad before he passed away. I sat him down one night and asked him how he would feel if I started IVF treatment, and we got pregnant whilst he was still with me. He burst into tears and told me it would be a dream come true. That was all I needed to hear, and the decision was made. I contacted the hospital the next day and made arrangements for our first appointment. John was determined to attend as many appointments as he could with me. Emma came with us so that she could help look after John and be ready to step in and take over if John wasn't able to attend any appointments. John thought it was great walking into our appointment with one woman on either side of him. He always said Emma was his second wife, and he knew how close we were and accepted when he married me, he was taking her on as well. As it turned out, Emma ended up attending all the appointments with me as John wasn't strong enough to go to them. I was concerned the stress of everything would be dangerous and affect our chances, but I was reassured that wouldn't be the case, and it was perfectly safe for us to do this, so my treatment began.

Those of you who have been through IVF treatment will know how hard it is both physically and mentality. My treatment was a course of thirty-five days of injections. First, I had to have internal scans to establish at what point in the month I was to start my treatment, and I also needed blood tests. As I was fortunate enough not to have any fertility problems, the process was fairly straightforward. I was very nervous with needles, so when it came to doing my first injection, I couldn't bring myself to do it. In stepped Emma, who was quite happy to show me how to do it. After that initial injection, I was able to do it myself. I got into my daily routine of treatment. Throughout my treatment, there were regular trips to the hospital for scans and blood tests.

Part way through my treatment John had a check-up with his neurosurgeon, who happily told us it looked like John had stabilised. We were over the moon. Was this due to our goal of getting pregnant? Who knew, but John had something to live for, and he was doing well.

So we continued to focus on IVF. I was so relieved when my body was finally ready for my eggs to be collected. I was bruised and tender from all the injections.

Following the egg collection, I was in a lot of pain and had to rest for a few days. I was exhausted. It had been a very emotional process, the variety of medication I'd had to take and the constant pressure I'd put on myself. Even though John was doing well, I still needed to get pregnant the first time. He needed to be part of the pregnancy and hopefully, be there for the birth.

A few days later, I was ready for insemination. Again Emma was by my side. How many friends can say they were there at the conception of their best friend's children? We thought this was hilarious, Emma made the whole process bearable. We joked about how the eggs would be inseminated with a turkey baster. The doctor asked if I wanted two eggs inseminating to give us a stronger chance of it working the first time. I agreed, I laughed at how I'd always wanted boy/girl twins since being a little girl and how amazing it would be if it actually happened.

Over the next few months, John's health was up and down. Some days, he was fine; other days, he was vomiting, and we had to call the nurses out. He took it all in his stride, as usual. He told me he knew he didn't have much longer but was not ready to go yet. We weren't pregnant yet.

It was now October, and John was starting to deteriorate fast. His breathing was becoming more shallow, and his Doctor told us we were looking at weeks now. He would go one of two ways, he'd go into a coma, and gradually his body would shut down until he stopped breathing, or he would have a brain haemorrhage. Neither would be painful. John wasn't scared, but he was scared of me watching him die and how I'd cope. I told him he didn't have a choice. I would be there till the very end. I was terrified I wouldn't be if I was asleep, but I knew I just had to be there.

Paul flew home from America a few days later. He wanted to spend some time with John while he could. John was so happy to see him, and he became stronger again. He wanted to spend time talking with his big brother. Paul had made some plans for John, and he had managed to arrange for John to be awarded his black belt in Karate. My brother had explained John's situation to his sensei, who had agreed John had earned his black belt. He may not have achieved it through conventional methods. However, he had shown the true strength of a warrior and, for that, had awarded John his black belt. John was ecstatic. A dream of his had come true. He didn't feel he had earned it properly, but when Paul explained why he had been awarded it, he felt happy and proud. His certificate was framed and hung with pride of place in our living room. His black belt would be put into a memory box containing everything about John for his children.

On the 9th of October 2012, we found out the IVF treatment had worked, and I was pregnant. I couldn't wait to tell John. By this point, he was on a lot of medication, so his first question was, "Is it a boy or a girl." He was so happy, and he knew he was a Dad. I was happy Paul was here to be part of this amazing moment for us both. We shared our news with our close friends and family. I'll never forget John smiling and saying, 'get in, my shit actually works!' we all laughed at this amazing moment. Toward the end of my brother's visit, John told me he wouldn't last another four weeks. I asked him why and he told me he just knew. I asked him to keep on fighting and take each day as it came.

After Paul left, John was exhausted and stopped getting out of bed. We had now hit the point where he was bedridden. He became distant at times. Whether this was him trying to protect me or the medication, I couldn't say I just made sure I was by his side as much as I could be. He told me he could feel pressure in his head, and he needed to keep fighting. He knew my viability scan was in three weeks, and then we'd know how my pregnancy was going. His Macmillan nurse could see he was deteriorating fast. He was sleeping twenty-two hours a day now and made some calls to try and bring my scan forward. It was brought forward, and I'd have it in a few days. John lost consciousness on the day of my scan. I went for my scan with Emma holding my hand and found out we were expecting twins. Twins, holy crap, this was huge. I had to tell John straight away. I rushed home. The nurses were with him. They told me he could hear me. I sat down beside him, held his hand, and told him our wonderful news. He grunted. They told me that was his way of letting me know he heard me. It was bittersweet, and this was supposed to be the best day of our lives. I was happy he knew his dream of being a Dad had come true. I hated that he'd never meet them and was terrified of how I would cope with two babies on my own.

On the 4th of November, I woke up to John showing signs of being in pain. I called the nurses, who came out immediately and gave him painkillers. It was time. The day before, they'd told me the time was coming for him to let go, so Emma had stayed with me throughout the night. I lay next to John, playing songs from our wedding. I cried and cuddled into him, knowing I had to say goodbye soon. That night I experienced a moment that I'll remember forever. I felt a hand stroke my face and the words 'I love you ' whispered in my ear. The voice and touch were my Mum's. I remembered it like it was yesterday. Some will say I was dreaming, imagining it as I was in such an emotional state, who knows, but I choose to believe it was my Mum comforting me and giving me strength at a time I needed it most. John's breathing started to slow down. I was by his side crying. I told him it was ok to let go, I would be ok, and that I loved him. With that, he took his final breath and passed away. It was excruciating watching my beloved husband die before my eyes. We all cried.

Everyone was contacted to let them know, and soon, our home was full of family coming to say their goodbyes to John. I tried to stand back and let everyone have their time with him. All I wanted to do was lie by his side and not let him go. By the afternoon, everyone had spent time with John, so I just lay with him crying. At some point, it all got too much for me, and denial set in. I went downstairs, telling everyone John wasn't really gone. He wouldn't have left me without saying goodbye. John's family pulled together around me to calm me down and comfort me. John's brother sat holding me until I calmed down. Eventually, they managed to make me sleep for a bit. When I woke, Emma was there, and I broke down. I knew he was really gone and wasn't coming back. Shortly after that, the undertakers came to take John away, and I watched him leave our home one last time, I had to see him leave. It killed me inside, but I knew I just had to do it. That night I saw the brightest star appear in the sky. To me, that was my John watching over me now and no longer suffering.

Chapter Six - The Final Goodbye

John and I had talked about his funeral, but he struggled to talk about what he really wanted, understandably. His only wish was that he had the song by The Calling, 'Wherever you go,' as he felt it expressed his thoughts about me. He also knew he wanted to be cremated. He didn't want his funeral to be sad. He wanted people to smile. He joked that he wanted everyone to be in fancy dress, dressed as superheroes. He was obsessed with Marvel, especially Spiderman.

When he passed away, I didn't know how I would manage to organise a funeral that would reflect who he was and whether I would make him proud. I used the Co-Op Funeral company, and I am so thankful I did, as Andrea, the Funeral Director, has remained a friend ever since. She also helped with my Dad's funeral. When I met with Andrea, John's brother was there to help. He kept me strong and helped me make decisions that would be good for John. When discussing his coffin, I joked about how great it would be if John had a Spiderman coffin. Andrea asked me to give her a minute to make a call. To my surprise, the phone call paid off, and John got his Spiderman coffin. I couldn't believe it. Due to John's amazing sense of humour, I knew he would be over the moon with it, and it would cause a great reaction from everyone who attended his funeral.

I then met with the lady who would conduct his service. She was lovely. We weren't religious people, so I felt a non-religious service was the best way to go. She agreed she would say some of the usual wording used in services, and I would write his eulogy. I asked his brother and sister and his best friends to put something together to add to my eulogy. With their input, I was able to write his eulogy describing the man he was, what he meant to other people and how much he would be missed.

The funeral was on Friday, the 9th of November, 2012, and this was yet another extremely hard day. I woke up with a sense of dread wondering whether I would be able to get through the day. I had arranged everything. The flowers were white calla lilies, just like our wedding flowers but with two red roses added to symbolise our miracle twin babies that were safely in my tummy. The music I picked with the help of his friends and brother, I picked two Linkin Park songs for the start of the service. They played Shadow of the day. The song is as though it is being sung by someone who has passed away, so it felt very appropriate. The second song was from me by Lifehouse, called From Where You Are. Again, the song seemed very appropriate as it describes losing someone and how you think about them. The third song was Linkin Park's Leave Out All The Rest. It's sung from the point of view of someone who has died and how they want to be remembered. The final song was The Calling, John's choice for me.

The hearse was leaving our home. I had been to see his coffin prior to the funeral, so I was prepared. But seeing it crippled me again, Emma came in the funeral car with John's family and me. As we travelled to the crematorium, I noticed people's reactions as we drove by. Seeing John's coffin made people's heads turn. He would've loved that. I hadn't told many people about his coffin as I wanted to see their reaction. When we arrived at the crematorium, there were over two hundred people standing outside. I was amazed at the number of people who had come to see him on his final journey. As we approached and people saw the coffin, everyone started clapping, and I could see smiles on their faces and knew I'd made the right decision. When I got out of the car, I could barely stand. My emotions took over and consumed me. The pain I was feeling was unbearable. I felt like my heart was literally breaking. Emma held me up and walked me into the crematorium. We sat down, ready for the service to commence. I had arranged for a large photo of John in his karate suit holding two children in the air above his head. I felt this picture showed his strength and his cheeky smile. I wanted a picture where everyone would look at him rather than down at the ground. The service went well except for a mix-up with the music, which I swear was John playing silly buggers and mixing it up to have his final say. Rather than flowers, I had asked for donations to Macmillan to say thank you for all their care and support for John and me. We raised an amazing amount of money through his service and a Justgiving page. We had a total of £1200, and I was over the moon with this.

When I announced John's funeral, I asked that everyone wear an item, whether it be clothing or accessories with superheroes on. To my amazement, everyone did. It made for an interesting gathering of people. I knew John would be smiling down, laughing at how ridiculous we all looked. I'd worn a pair of John's Spiderman boxer shorts and socks.

There were so many people at the funeral it was hard to speak to everyone. There were childhood friends of John's, work colleagues, and people from his adult life. Friends of mine came to support me, along with some of my work colleagues. I was amazed by how much support I had.

After the service, we went to the Shuttle and Loom, our local pub, for the wake. His Mum had sorted out all the food and done a great job. The wake turned out to be really good. People were talking and drinking. It was great hearing stories about John and how people knew him and remembered him. I ended up leaving early. I was exhausted and, by this point, nine weeks pregnant, trying to hide why I wasn't drinking as only a handful of people knew I was pregnant at this point.

I went home and reflected on the day I had said my final goodbye to my husband. I felt I had done him proud. I looked through our Facebook pages, and over the week of his passing, both our pages had been inundated with messages and posts of condolences and shared memories. I ended up putting together a tribute book for our children for when they would be old enough to read through them. It would show them how much their Dad was loved and help them learn more about the man he was.

From that day on, it was just our babies and me. I knew John was with us, watching over us. Our very own Guardian Angel.

Chapter Seven – Letting Go

When your whole future is taken away from you, how do you even begin to come to terms with that, let alone find a way to get through each day? The funeral was over, and I was Ten weeks pregnant with twins, what was I supposed to do now? I had another thirty weeks just me and my ever-growing bump to get my head around losing John. I knew I had to be strong and look after myself for the sake of my babies.

Everywhere I looked in the house, there were reminders of John. I hadn't slept in our bed since he passed away, and I couldn't even get in it, that was where he had died. It hurt so much just to look at it. So that was the first thing to sort out, I needed a new bed. Once the new bed arrived, I was able to go back to sleeping in our bedroom, I had slept in the spare room since he passed, but that didn't feel right.

The next step was going through the process of making sure all the relevant people were notified, including his bank and his employer. Even though he'd been terminally ill, his employer hadn't ended his contract. I had to go in and complete paperwork with the HR department. That was hard seeing his work colleagues, seeing the sadness in their eyes when they looked at me, and being handed a box with his belongings from his desk.

I had to inform Revenue and Customs of his passing and also that I was his widow, pregnant with his children. This meant I was entitled to benefits to support his children and me. It felt so wrong getting this financial help, but I had to face the facts I was going to need all the support I could get to raise our children. I have to say the people I dealt with were so empathetic and didn't make me feel uncomfortable.

So now the formalities were out of the way, I was able to focus on facing our home. I knew I had to go through his clothes and belongings. I didn't know what I would find and was very apprehensive about doing it. I went through his clothes first, Emma helped me do this. I knew if I did it on my own, I would keep everything. We had to organise everything, piles for charity, piles to throw out, and piles to keep. I'd pick items up, remembering the last time he wore it and what we were doing. He had so many clothes, some that I'd never even seen him wear and some that I couldn't believe he even had in the first place. As John was such a superhero fan, I'd bought him numerous superhero t-shirts over the years. Not a chance I was parting with them, so I started piling them up. Sixteen t-shirts later, I had a nice neat pile of geek t-shirts. They have been packed away in a box to be opened in years to come. I decided to keep his leather jacket, and I wasn't ready to part with that yet. His dressing gown was also staying put, and I had started wearing that every night after he died. He even had a pair of Scooby Doo slippers, and I have no idea why but I couldn't bin them. They were given to one of his nieces. Among his things, I found the speech he made at our wedding, along with the flower from his buttonhole. I couldn't believe he'd kept it. Reading his speech brought back memories of our happy day, the emotions were so strong my heart ached for just one more day with my husband.

As John was a big gamer, he had his own games room, and I had to go through all of his games. These were shared out between his nephews and friends.

I was faced with the little things like his favourite mug, little things lying around the house, and his toothbrush. Moving his toothbrush was actually the hardest thing to let go of. Who'd have thought a toothbrush would be so hard to put in the bin? In my eyes, whilst John's toothbrush was sitting in the cup on the bathroom window sill, I wasn't alone. It wasn't just me in the house. Crazy, I know, but it brought me comfort. That toothbrush stayed there until several months after the twins were born. Looking back, I know I kept it far too long, it wasn't exactly hygienic keeping it, but in the eyes of a grieving widow, you do what you have to cope.

I wanted a way that I could keep John close to me at all times. I'd never heard of Ashes into Glass before, so when I heard what they could do with the ashes of a loved one, I knew I needed to look into it. I looked through their website at the various products they could make that incorporated a loved one's ashes. I finally settled upon having a ring made, I wanted a red one for our birthstone Ruby, and inside I wanted the words 'love you for eternity' engraved. Off went my order with the teaspoon of ashes they had asked for, I knew it would take time for them to make the ring, so I patiently waited. The day the ring arrived I was so excited to see it, I opened the box and burst into tears when I saw how beautiful it was. I put it straight on and instantly felt comforted.

After a few days, I decided to send an email to the company thanking them for the beautiful ring and how much it meant to me. I explained the story of John and me and how much comfort it had already brought me. A few days later, I received a response to my email from the company. They thanked me for my feedback and asked if I'd be willing to let them post it on their Facebook page with a photo of John and me. I thought, why not? They gave me my beautiful ring. They posted our wedding photo and my feedback, and I was blown away by the response it received from all around the world. People were commenting, sending their love and best wishes to me and the twins, and they were moved by our story. The post reached nearly fifty thousand people around the world. I could not believe how one feedback email could move so many people. John would've smiled at that and joked about being famous.

From the last few months of John's life and several years after he passed, I had the continuous support of a Counsellor from the local hospice St Teresa's. Julie, my Counsellor, was a lovely lady. She helped me process everything that was happening. I was able to say every single thought and emotion I was feeling without the fear of judgement or upsetting anyone. I released so much anger and raw emotions in those sessions that I lost count of the hours I spent crying with Julie. I had 'survivor's guilt'. Why did I get to carry on with my life, and John's was taken away from him? He was a good person. Who decides who should live and who should die? So many questions that no one could answer. Although Julie couldn't give me answers, she helped me really look at the emotions and questions I had. She made me realise that knowing the answers wouldn't make any difference. If anything, they'd probably make me feel worse. Over the years, Julie helped me in so many ways, gave me guidance when I needed it, and, most of all, enabled me to grieve in my own way. There are not enough words to express my gratitude to her. My journey would have been exceptionally harder without her.

In the months that followed, I decided to make a memory box, this box would bring comfort to me and also enable me to teach our children about their Dad. I ordered a beautiful wooden box and had a silver plaque put on the lid saying 'John's Memory Box'. I put the wedding speech and flower from his buttonhole in it, along with his black karate belt, his favourite mug, favourite t-shirt, photos, cufflinks I'd bought him for our Wedding day, the eulogy from his funeral, and a CD with the songs that were played. I also put his aftershave and deodorant in, that way, I'd always be able to remember his smell. As John had collected superhero figurines over the years, I also put one of those in the memory box. This box has brought comfort to me so many times, and I know it's always there whenever I need it.

The first Christmas was awful, and I was dreading it. I'd had lots of offers to spend Christmas with various friends and family. But I didn't want that. I wanted Christmas in our home, just me and my bump. I'd bought a Marks and Spencers Christmas Dinner for one, so I'd still get my Christmas Dinner. I had a quiet day thinking about the last few years, thinking about what the future would've been like if John had never gotten cancer. And I tried to picture what the future was going to be like, just the twins and me. I cried so much that day, but one part of the day produced tears of happiness that I will always treasure. In the evening, I was lying on the sofa watching the TV, and I suddenly felt a strange sensation in my stomach. 'That couldn't have been a kick, could it' I thought. I rested my hands on my stomach and waited patiently, and there it was again another strange feeling. My babies were kicking, I started talking to them, and more kicks followed. Tears of happiness rolled down my cheeks, I had been given a Christmas gift from John. My babies were letting me know I wasn't alone and never would be again.

Over the years, I have joined Facebook groups for widows and support groups to try and find a way to move forward. One of the most helpful things I did was join a group called 'Second Firsts', which was set up by a lady who had experienced love and loss herself. Christina Rasmussen became my unofficial guide to grieving. I bought her book and started reading, and it helped me understand the journey I was on, from sitting in the 'waiting room' as she called it, to finding my 'survivor'. There were exercises in the book, like forms of meditation, to help. One exercise I did I remember so clearly, I had to clear my mind completely and walk through a door, I had no idea what was on the other side. As I walked through the door, I stepped into a beautiful meadow. There were my children running around with a black Labrador, and in the distance was a tall, dark-haired man watching. I couldn't see his face but knew he was waiting to be invited in. I dismissed the vision and carried on with the book. At that point in my journey, I firmly believed I would never love another man or even want one. Little did I know that vision would come back to me in years to come. Christina also sent weekly emails called 'message in a bottle', these emails often described how I was feeling. They showed me that someone else understood the pain I was going through. I looked forward each week to receiving these.

Christina went on to write another book called 'Where Did you Go'. I read this in later years, and again this book helped me immensely. I'm quite open-minded when it comes to spirituality, so I was open to the idea of being able to connect with John. This book would enable me to do just that. It took a lot of focus and practice, but eventually, through visualisation exercises, I connected with John. I got to say the burning things I'd wanted to say to him for months. I had spent many nights talking to John in the early days of losing him, hoping he could hear me. But with these exercises, I was able to hear his response. Now, I know some people will think what a load of rubbish, and others will believe, either way, it doesn't matter. What does matter is that it helped me, it brought me comfort, and it brought me strength. I felt stronger, and John had let me know I was doing a good job, he was proud of me and loved me. No one else could've given me that, it was exactly what I needed to move another step forward.

In later years I decided the time had come to scatter John's ashes, he'd been sitting in a scatter tube in our living room since the day I brought him home, and it comforted me to have him there with me.

I thought long and hard about where I wanted to scatter him, where his final resting place should be. Originally I wanted to take him back to the Grand Canyon, but I knew the likelihood of being able to do this was slim to none. So I thought about where in England would be a good replacement, then I thought back to our last trip away together. Windermere, what better place! We loved it there, and we'd had so many conversations about what our lives would've been like if John hadn't become ill. Windermere was definitely the perfect place. I drove there one day and took him to lake Windermere. I found a nice, calm, and peaceful spot and scattered John's ashes. As I watched his ashes float away to his final resting place, I felt a moment of calmness and acceptance wash over me. He wasn't coming back, and it was time for me to start looking to the future. The future for our children and me.

Four years after losing John, I decided I wanted to go and see a clairvoyant. I was sceptical but hopeful they would be able to give me something to help me move forward. Emma was happy to come along and see what they could tell her, too, so we booked our appointments to see someone who'd been recommended to us.

It turned out to be an experience I will never forget, the things this guy knew it wasn't possible for him to know. He knew John had been taken away from me, and he said John was standing behind me from the moment I walked through the door. I felt myself looking over my shoulder at that point. He knew what had happened to him, the details of his passing, and what I did with the flowers for his funeral. He knew I was raising the twins alone, and he even knew their characters. I was Mum and Dad, and John said I was doing a fantastic job. He told me John was sorry as he didn't want to leave me. He gave me so much detail about my and John's relationship and the way he expressed things, it was done in the same way John would've said it. He even included that I wore trousers in our relationship. This made me laugh, as John always wanted me to be happy. He'd have given me the world if he could. It was an extremely emotional and moving experience. I'm glad I did it, at that point in my life, I still needed reassurance. Reassurance from John that he was happy with the way I was raising our children, reassurance he had been by my side watching over us. Whether you believe it or not, an experience like that can give you the comfort and answers you need to keep putting one foot in front of the other.

When you are grieving, you do what you need to to survive, all the well-meaning sympathetic comments in the world mean nothing when all you want to do is scream, 'he's gone, and it's not fair'. I have friends who have unfortunately had to go through the heartache of losing their partner, too, as someone who gets it, I have made sure I have offered my support to them. Some I have had long conversations with and helped them regain their strength to get through each day. Being able to talk to someone who has walked in your shoes, so to speak, really helps. I was fortunate to find that when I started my journey, without that, I think I would've found things a lot harder.

Chapter Eight - Health and Operations

Now I class myself as a healthy person, but six operations before the age of forty are taking the mick, and not one of them resulted in any enhancements!

Operation one was to remove a growth from the base of my spine. I'd been bitten by a mosquito on holiday in Greece a few years prior to this, and a lump had formed. I was convinced something had laid an egg in me, and when they cut me open, they would witness a scene similar to the film Alien. As the growth had become painful, I needed an operation to remove it. I had a local anaesthetic and remembered asking during surgery whether they'd removed an insect. Thankfully it wasn't that. It turned out to be a lump of fat. This made no sense at the time as there was barely any fat on me, but I was thankful that's all it was.

Operation two, now I am a clumsy person, so this one was the result of an accident at work where I got my foot trapped in a revolving door. I roll my eyes just thinking about it now. At the time, I had just damaged my toe, or so I thought. After having severe knee pain for several months, I finally gave in and visited my Doctor. After being referred to a specialist, I ended up having knee surgery to release a nerve that was getting trapped behind my kneecap. I was left with three tiny scars and now know when the weather's going to change as my knee starts to throb.

Operations three and four were the result of yet another accident. This time, I slipped in the shower, landing on the base of my spine. After weeks of pain, I visited my Doctor and was put on painkillers. Three years later, my pain was getting worse, so I was given an MRI scan. This showed I'd dislocated a disc, and my coccyx bone was stuck in one position, causing extreme pain every time I sat down. My first back operation resulted in a disc being removed, and a titanium cage was put in to hold my spine in place. The pain was awful, my wound had been stapled, and I had to go through intensive physio to help get me back to full movement again. I was on morphine patches and several tablets to manage my pain. The morphine affected my concentration and made me lethargic at times.

Several months passed, and I was still struggling. After seeing my consultant, it was decided I needed a further operation to remove my coccyx bone. This would enable me to sit down without being in pain. The official term for this condition is coccidia, in simple terms, 'chronic pain in the ass', which is quite appropriate for me. This operation was a difficult one to recover from. I had to go to the hospital daily for the first few days to get my dressings changed. It takes longer for this area of the body to heal, and the risk of infection is high, so I had to be very careful and look after myself. I also had to sit on a rubber ring as I was in so much pain. Eventually, I healed and was able to start moving around more and try to get my fitness levels back up. I've always been conscious of my fitness levels, and not being able to go to the gym and work out hit me hard. I became quite depressed during this time. Eventually, I pulled myself out of it and got my head back in the game, and started working out again. I've never been able to work out as I did prior to surgery, but I've always managed to keep my fitness levels fairly high and look after myself.

Operation five was a fairly common and standard operation for a lot of women. I had endometriosis and needed the cysts removed from my ovaries. This was keyhole surgery, and was in and out in a day. Very straightforward, and after a few days, I was back to normal and had fully recovered from the surgery.

Each scar on my body tells a story. John always told me scars were cool, so I wore mine with pride.

Chapter Nine – Norman

Operation six, now this was a big one and one I certainly didn't expect. During John's illness, I suffered from numbness on the left-hand side of my face and loss of hearing. The Doctors put this down to stress, given the circumstances I was dealing with. Shortly after John passed away, I changed medical practice and registered with his Doctor. I am so thankful I did. When I told him my symptoms and that it had been going on for a year, he told me hearing loss should always be investigated and referred me to the Ear, Nose, and Throat department to be reviewed.

The consultant arranged for a CT scan as they were unable to do an MRI scan due to me being in the first trimester of my pregnancy. I was not prepared for what I was told when they called me back in to discuss the results. They told me I had a brain tumour. I thought it was some sick joke. I'd just lost John to a brain tumour. Now I'm being told I have one. Give me a break! They explained mine was an acoustic neuroma (a tumour in the ear canal). This type of tumour was non-malignant, thankfully. But I would need treatment, so I was referred to a Neurosurgeon.

My Neurosurgeon was a lovely man. I had an MRI scan prior to my first meeting with him. He needed to know exactly what was happening with the tumour. Luckily I was in the second trimester of my pregnancy, so it was safer to do a scan. In my appointment, he explained my tumour was small and that it would be monitored. Whilst I was pregnant, he couldn't do much, but it would need removing as it was 4.5cm in size. He wanted to get me to 32 weeks in my pregnancy, if possible, before he operated. This would be safer for the twins. He would consult with my Obstetrician to decide what was best for me and whether I could have a natural birth or whether the strain of pushing would be too dangerous for me.

Unfortunately, all decisions were taken out of my hands. On Monday, the 11th of February, 2013, I was admitted to the hospital due to having severe headaches. After consultation, it was confirmed I was experiencing neurological changes that were becoming dangerous and meant that I had to have surgery to remove my tumour and soon. Initially, my neurosurgeon wasn't keen on doing the long procedure and chose the shorter procedure as it would be safer for the babies. I was only 23 weeks pregnant. If anything went wrong, he would only be able to save me and not my babies.

On Thursday, the 14th, I underwent seven hours of brain surgery. The shorter procedure wasn't an option. I was terrified in the morning and had barely slept, worrying about whether my babies would survive. As they wheeled me into the theatre, I felt a calmness come over me. John was there. I could feel his presence. I was going to be ok. I woke up later that day to find I was completely deaf in my left ear, my left eye wouldn't close, and my face was paralysed on the left side. I looked like I'd had a stroke. In my eyes, I was hideous, a freak. How could I function like this? Then I realised I had to, my babies had survived, and they needed me. My neurosurgeon managed to remove 95% of the tumour and told me at a later date, I would have treatment to kill the remaining tumour. He was happy with how my surgery went. My paralysis would be temporary. Unfortunately, my hearing loss would be permanent.

I was discharged from the hospital after a couple of days, but I wasn't allowed to be on my own. My brother Paul was flying home from America to look after me for a week but couldn't get home for a couple of days. Therefore Emma stepped up yet again to come and stay with me. I was so grateful but also concerned. Now Emma is great at many things, but cooking is not one of them. We joked about what she would feed me and the risk I was taking of being poisoned. If I remember rightly, Emma's husband gave her instructions on what to make me and how to do it. She did a great job in the end. When Paul arrived, I was over the moon. Not only would I be having lovely meals cooked for me, but I was also getting to spend some quality time with him. He supported me in building my strength and independence again.

As I'm sure, you can imagine staying positive after all that I had been through the last couple of years was hard. But I had to be strong. I decided naming my tumour would help me, that's when I truly acknowledged 'Norman' and what had actually happened to me. 'Norman Neuroma' has changed me in ways I never thought would happen, some good, some bad.

My road to recovery has been a long one, with yearly check-ups and scans. I have had intense physiotherapy and been hooked up to a tens machine daily to encourage the nerves to regrow and function to return to my face.

Regular appointments with an eye specialist as my left eye doesn't produce tears and wouldn't close. I couldn't smile for seven months. Even then, it was barely a smile. I'd always had a huge smile that would take over my face when I was happy. Now I didn't look like me at all, I'd never been a vain person, but to lose my face, my identity, I didn't know how I was supposed to come to terms with this. Yet again, I'd been robbed of something, and I was so angry.

I had to drink through a straw as my mouth would not close on the left side, which would often result in me dribbling. This was very embarrassing. Eating made me feel revolted as I couldn't close my mouth fully. I would put my hand in front of my mouth so no one could see me eat. The only way to describe how I thought I looked was like a cow chewing grass. I was mortified and avoided eating in front of people. I could only eat on the right side of my mouth, and if I tried to eat on the left side, I would end up biting my cheek, and due to not being able to feel it would end up with a mouth full of blood. I had to really concentrate and learn a new way of eating and drinking. Over time both have improved, although I still can't eat on my left side and will cover my face when eating in front of people. Drinking is easier as I can drink from a glass now, but from a bottle can be difficult if the lid isn't the right shape for me. It's often easier to hold the left side of my mouth shut with my fingers to avoid the risk of dribbling. I don't think I'll ever stop feeling self-conscious.

I couldn't wear make-up for the first three years, for some women, that is a big deal, and to me, it was. I'd always loved make-up, I used to do fancy eye make-up every day. Now I couldn't even put any make-up near my eyes for risk of causing an infection. Another part of expressing myself was taken away, and I couldn't even use makeup to disguise the flaws that were now visible to everyone. This added to the feelings of being disgusting, and I tried so hard to hide my face.

I have worked hard for nine years to get to where I am now, and I have regained some function in my face. To passers-by, you wouldn't know I had paralysis, people who know me and know what has happened to me tell me you can't tell there's anything wrong with my face. Whereas I am constantly aware of it. The lack of sensation, the need to put eye drops in regularly throughout the day to stop my eye from hurting, and wearing a hearing aid so that I can hold a conversation. I still struggle with my hearing, especially in noisy places. I tend to lip-read where possible. I have adapted to this way of life, and it doesn't hold me back as much as it did in the early days. I had sessions with a psychologist to help me see myself in a more positive way. For a few years, I avoided mirrors and getting my photo taken as all I could see was a freak. I was paranoid that people were staring at me when I walked past them.

I had lip fillers done a couple of times to level out my mouth, so it wasn't as obvious that it drooped at one side. As much as this boosted my confidence, I couldn't justify the cost several times a year. I had appointments to discuss having Botox to level out my face, if I was to go ahead with it, I would need it done in a theatre in a hospital due to the areas and amount of Botox I would need, and it would need to be done every six months. Now, this was approved to be done on the NHS for the rest of my life, at no cost to myself. Great I could improve how I looked at the detriment of losing movement in areas of my face that was fine. This made me think long and hard about why I was considering going threw with it. I realised I was doing it for all the wrong reasons, and I was more concerned with what other people thought when they looked at me. Why was the opinion of complete strangers so important to me? Honestly, I couldn't come up with one good reason why other people's opinions mattered.

Eventually, I realised I didn't look hideous. I am beautiful inside and out, no matter what anyone thinks. I'm a survivor and always will be. My recovery is still ongoing, but I'm hopeful that one day I will fully regain feeling in my face again. I've been told that my recovery has surpassed the expectations of my medical team and the functionality that people with my condition normally achieve. I think that's because I'm so stubborn and don't like being told I can't do something. I get days where I can't stand to look at myself and feel anger and frustration at what has been taken away from me, but then the survivor voice inside me steps in and tells me to quit the pity party. I'm alive.

Norman is still in situ, but he's no longer in control. He still gives me the occasional moment of panic when I get a really bad headache, but logic soon sets in, telling me not to worry.

Operation seven, well, that one will be explained in the next chapter.

Chapter Ten - Pregnancy and Birth

As you already know, I became pregnant with twins by IVF during John's illness. As I mentioned earlier, from being a small child, I always wanted boy/girl twins. So when I found out, I was expecting twins, and they were boy/girl twins, well, you can imagine my amazement. Yes, I knew there was a good chance it would happen, given that they were IVF babies and two eggs had been inseminated to give us a good chance of getting pregnant. So yes, when the viability scan showed twins, I was over the moon. It was a miracle. Then reality hit, 'Oh wow, I was going to have two babies and be raising them as a single mother.' So many thoughts went through my head, how would I manage with two babies? Will I be enough for them? Have I done the right thing bringing them into the world knowing their father would not be with us? How will I provide for them? Could I even manage to have a job and be a full-time parent? All these would eventually be answered. For now, I had to focus on keeping healthy to ensure my pregnancy had no complications and they were safely brought into the world.

I referred to the twins as my 'ninja babies '. They'd survived my brain surgery, so the title was fitting. My two strong, resilient miracle babies.

Throughout my pregnancy, Emma was by my side, attending appointments with me and giving me advice (she was in the final year of her Midwifery course, so she was the perfect person to hold my hand), reassuring me I could do this. Emma was my rock, as always. I could not have gotten through all that I have without her. In fact, several months later, I nominated her for the Tommy Angel Award because of everything she had done for me. She couldn't believe I'd done this, and we joked about imagining if she was shortlisted, as it turned out, she was shortlisted. This resulted in me going to Leeds to be interviewed and telling the story of Emma and me and how our friendship is unlike no other. We still didn't think she would win. We imagined the other candidates' stories would be more worthy. Then I received the call we never expected, and she had won! Emma actually won the award, I was so proud of her, and she was amazed. She 100% deserved to win. Unfortunately, we weren't able to attend the presentation ceremony in London, Emma was completing her final exams, and I had new-born babies to look after. To receive the award was enough for Emma, and when it finally arrived, we were so happy. An award that shows a friendship like ours is rare and should be treasured. To this day, Emma would say she only did what any good friend would do. In my eyes, she went above and beyond. I will never be able to repay her, but she knows she means the world to me and is family, Auntie to my children, and like a sister to me.

So back to my pregnancy, when I found out I had a tumour, I became a high-risk pregnancy which meant I needed regular scans to monitor how my babies were doing. They, thankfully, were growing perfectly and gave me a very neat little bump. I didn't really suffer from morning sickness. I didn't get weird cravings. On the whole, I had a very good pregnancy if you ignore the whole brain tumour thing.

Once I'd had my tumour removed, I was able to focus on trying to carry the twins to full term. My due date was the 12th of June. I was 23 weeks over halfway through and working on my recovery from my operation but was restricted from using any machines to help because of the pregnancy.

The twins had different ideas about when they wanted to come out! At 31 weeks and 5 days, they decided to let me know this. I woke up one morning, and my bed was soaked. I thought this was strange so I phoned Emma thinking this was normal and maybe I'd been too hot. Emma calmly told me I had to call the labour ward and tell them what had happened, as it appeared my waters had broken. So I made the call thinking, 'My waters haven't broken. I'll probably just be told to rest or something'. No, that was not the case, they told me I had to go to the hospital, and they wanted to check me over. So I called Emma back and told her, she told me to pack a bag and she'd be straight round. I'd just got out of the shower. My hair was soaking wet. When I asked if I had time to dry my hair, she firmly told me 'no and to get my arse ready.' Me, still thinking nothing was happening, did as I was told and was ready when Emma arrived. Off we went, me not really thinking about what was happening, and Emma (as I later found out) was panicking inside and not letting on to me at all.

I was so lucky with the consultant I had. He was a lovely man and sounded exactly like Sean Connery, which made me laugh. I was given a check-up and told my waters had broken and that I was in the early stages of labour. Holy crap, ninja babies were on their way, and I'm going to have two babies soon. My head was all over, panicking it was too soon, I wasn't ready, I couldn't do this. Emma stayed with me most of the day, keeping me company and calm. When she went home, I knew I had to try and get some rest ready for what could potentially be a long few days depending on how my labour went.

I remember waking in the middle of the night in so much pain. I begged the midwives to call Emma. I was scared. They knew Emma through her placement during her course. They knew what she'd say to me and reassured me my labour pains were normal, and they'd call her in the morning. Morning couldn't come soon enough as far as I was concerned. I'd rather go through brain surgery again than the pain I was feeling!

Now with Emma being in the final year of her midwifery course, she had already delivered a few babies. There is a line that must be drawn in a Friendship, and we had reached the point where that line must not be crossed. I told Emma in no uncertain terms she stays next to my head during the birth, and she does not venture past my stomach. We were extremely close but not close enough for her to be viewing my downstairs area. We laughed our heads off at the fact we were even having this conversation, and obviously, she 100% agreed with me.

Finally, morning came, I'd managed to get a few hours of sleep, and Emma turned up fairly early. My consultant reviewed me and decided the babies were coming and that I'd need a C-section. I was gutted. I wanted a natural birth even though I knew the pain would be worse than I'd already experienced. I just knew I wanted a natural birth, especially as their conception hadn't been natural way. But obviously, I didn't have a choice. It had been discussed how I would give birth, given that part of my tumour was still there. Initially, it was thought I'd have to be put to sleep as the pressure in my brain could be dangerous to the babies and me. After much discussion between my consultant and Neurosurgeon, it was decided a natural birth would be possible, but as you now know, that wasn't an option anymore.

At 31 weeks and 6 days, on the 16th of April, my babies made their entrance. At 11:07, Archie John was born weighing 2lbs 12oz, and at 11:10, Ella Kate was born weighing 3lbs 12oz. I'd known from my 20-week scan my dream of a boy and a girl had come true, but them being born and physically being with me was amazing. Their birth wasn't an easy one. I remember there were around 16 people in the room. I had an epidural. I remember the table being tilted as I became very lightheaded and didn't feel well. I also found out later my uterus had turned inside out as Ella was born, and there was a fair bit of blood. The main thing was we were all ok. Archie and Ella were taken straight to Special Care to be checked over, with them being premature and so tiny, they would need to spend some time there. At this point, I hadn't seen my babies. Emma had, and she told me they were beautiful. I went into recovery and, within half an hour, started expressing my milk. It was important my babies had this as it would help them get stronger quicker.

I was wheeled around to see them once they were settled in. They looked so tiny, like little dolls in their incubators. They were both little jaundice, so they had their eyes covered and the special lamps on them, I was able to put my hand in and touch them. I was scared to touch them because they looked so delicate. I got to hold them the next day. It felt incredible to finally hold these little people that had been growing inside me for 7 months. They were perfect, and I knew we'd be ok. I spent as much time as I could with them whilst regaining my strength after my C-section (operation number seven!). I was discharged after a week but obviously couldn't drive. I hated being away from them. I'm their Mum. I should be with them, was all I could think, but I did as I was told. John's Dad drove me to the hospital every day, so I could be with them, and he would come and pick me up every evening.

They were in special care for six weeks in total, Ella could've come home after 4 weeks, but I didn't want to separate them. The nurses were amazing. They talked to me about how they were doing, reassured me, and taught me how to look after them. Initially, they were fed my milk through a tube in their nose, but as they grew stronger, I was then able to breastfeed. I was so desperate to do this as this was the last natural part of having a child I could do for them. I was so thankful I managed it. I held them like rugby balls and learnt how to dual feed them.

Whilst they were in special care, I raised the question of whether they would inherit mine or John's brain tumours. As it turned out, John's was not hereditary. However, there was a chance mine was if I carried the NF2 gene. Thankfully I was able to have a test done to see if I did, and thankfully it came back negative. The twins were also given brain scans to ensure everything was ok, and again, thankfully, everything was fine. The relief I felt was unreal. I'd never have forgiven myself if they'd inherited my condition. If I'd known I had the tumour before I got pregnant, I wouldn't have gone ahead with the pregnancy.

Finally, Archie was strong enough to come out of his incubator and be moved to another room. By this time, we'd developed a nice little routine for our day. I would read stories to them, play them music, have cuddles with them, basically anything to help me bond with them. I also started playing them the same song at the end of each day, 'Goodnight Sweetheart' by the Overtures.

For the final week in special care, I moved into the hospital into one of the rooms they had for parents preparing to take their babies home from special care. We lived in that room, me caring for them and the nurses checking on us regularly throughout the day and night.

We finally came home at the end of May. When we got home, I just stood there, and I didn't have a clue what to do. It soon started to fall into place.

Chapter Eleven - Recovery

Once the twins were home, I was able to get us into a nice routine and also begin my recovery from my paralysis. As the twins were in special care for six weeks, it meant I'd recovered from my C-section.

Initially, I focussed on working out what our routine would be and how I would manage to look after two babies on my own and focus on my own rehabilitation. The first few months were spent getting our routine going, monitoring their progress, and sleeping whenever I could.

As they were premature and Archie had been born with several medical problems, it meant regular appointments with his various specialists and visits from the Health Visitor to ensure I was coping with new-borns and being a first-time Mum. They were weighed regularly, and I kept a detailed log of all their feeds, naps, and routine. Archie had an ophthalmologist to monitor the Coloboma in his left eye and a specialist for his heart as he had a missing value and two holes in his heart. He also had an Occupational Therapist and Physiotherapist that monitored his mobility. It became apparent that his left hand hadn't formed in the correct way. We later found out he had a rare condition called 'Windblown Hand

Syndrome' in his left hand, which resulted in his fingers leaning to one side and the webbing between his fingers attached up to his first knuckles. He was later referred to a plastic surgeon who operated, which resulted in him having more mobility in his hand. He's still reviewed yearly and will have further operations as he grows. Amazingly he's left-handed, and his condition does not stop him from being able to do what other children his age can do. He's a brave little boy.

Once we had settled into our routine, I started seeing a Physiotherapist to help me regain functionality in my face. She worked with me, giving me exercises to do, and eventually suggested I start using a tens machine to provide nerve stimulation which in time helped waken my nerves, enabling some function to return.

It has been a long process, and I am still recovering. I was told initially that it was highly unlikely I would regain full function again. Throughout my recovery, I have been determined to prove everyone wrong and regain my face. So far, I have exceeded their expectations, and nine years on, I am still making progress.

As I mentioned previously, my face drooped on one side, making me look like I had had a stroke. It took six months before I had a hint of a smile. I found this extremely difficult every mother wants photos with their new-born baby, so obviously, I wanted photos too. However, I refused to have photos taken. If anyone ever managed to catch a picture, the left side of my face was always hidden. I regret not having more photos taken with my babies, but when I look at the photos that were taken, I go straight back to how I was back then and how I felt. It's painful remembering how I looked and felt, and it has caused years of emotional distress.

There were a lot of dark times for me when I felt I wasn't good enough for the twins and how I'd embarrassed them because of how I looked. Every time I went out, I felt like people were staring at me, and I could see looks of pity in people's eyes. Someone once said to me that I looked like my face was melting, that comment has stayed with me and, unfortunately, did a lot of damage to my confidence. When I was out, I would try and hide my face, and I'd wear big sunglasses to cover my eyes not only to protect them from the light and wind but also to avoid eye contact with people. I felt hideous, and seeing the looks of pity, and sometimes disgust was soul-destroying. It was hard enough getting the pity looks when people found out I was a widow but adding how I looked made me feel ten times worse. People would ask how I was doing, I knew they were being nice, but inside I felt like they were waiting for me to crack and were just being nosy. I thought people always thought, 'Poor girl, look at how her life has turned out, a single mother, who's going to love her looking like that.' I know this was just me projecting my own feelings. I felt no one would ever love me, I was a freak, and nothing anyone said could change that.

It's taken a lot of hard work to get to where I am now. I still struggle with my confidence, but I now know people can not see what I class as my flaws anymore. Yes, I am reminded every day that I have paralysis. I still don't have full feeling in my cheek, my lips aren't even anymore, and my eye doesn't blink as fast as my other eye and dries out a lot. But I'm more like the old me now and am continuing to get stronger every day.

My children don't know about my tumour. I decided not to tell them, mainly because they were too young to understand but also because I didn't want them to think I was going to die. They know their Dad died because of brain cancer, and I don't want them to think the same will happen to them. When they are old enough, they will be told the truth. That is partly why I have written this book. I want them to know my journey and how they saved my life by being born. They gave me a reason to carry on, a reason to fight to recover, and a reason to go from almost broken to whole again. They taught me how to smile again, love again, and live again. I will be eternally grateful to them. Our bond is strong and always will be.

Chapter Twelve - Raising Twins

Where do you begin when you're given two babies at once? You learn every day. You learn to split yourself in two and multitask whilst keeping two babies happy. I believed I had to do everything for them and shouldn't ask for help as I had to be able to cope on my own. Don't get me wrong, I had plenty of people around me keeping me sane, checking if I needed anything, and offering constant support and help. Even knowing I could phone any one of my friends for help, I didn't unless I really couldn't cope. I remember calling Emma one evening crying as I couldn't get them to settle, and they were both screaming. Emma, as always, came straight to my side and helped me settle them both and got them to sleep.

Even when the twins came home, they were still so small, and they wore tiny baby clothes. One day I decided to see if a 'Build-A-Bear' costume would fit them. To my amazement, they did, so I dressed them both in karate suits with black belts on. I laid them on a black mat and took their photo. This is one of my all-time favourite photos of them. I have no idea what possessed me to see if the costumes would fit, but I'm glad I did. There was another time when I laid a large bottle of Jack Daniels whiskey in their crib with them, and it was actually bigger than them. This showed how tiny they were, but it's also a great reminder of how far they've come.

I was lucky. A few months after the twins were born, Paul and his family came to visit from America for a few weeks. They helped so much, cooking meals for me, helping with feeding, bathing, and getting them settled in bed. Even getting up during the night to help with the night feeds. During their visit, I got to recharge and have a few days out as one big family. When they returned home, my house felt so empty, but this was my life, me and the kids.

At about four months old, they started sleeping through the night, which was a huge blessing for me. I was able to have some time to myself in the evening and get a good night's sleep. I started using the E.A.S.Y routine with them (East, Activity, Sleep, You). I followed this religiously every day, and it worked wonders. We had a fantastic routine. I spent quality time with them playing on the play mat, using sensory toys, singing songs, and cuddling. The early stages are so important. I knew this and needed to do it well. I started taking them to playgroups and made some new friends. I had a social life again. Ok, it was nothing like my old social life, but I was getting out, and it did us all good. I was guaranteed adult conversation and compared notes with my new Mum friends. I'd got myself another support network. To this day, I still have contact with some of them. One of them went on to become the twins' childminder. They adore her, and she loves them.

As I live in my childhood home, I've been very fortunate to have the support of my neighbours. Some of them have known me since I was a child and knew the events of my life. When the twins came along, they were so happy to meet them and watch them grow up too. I know which neighbours I can go to whenever I need help. They always stop to talk to me and the twins and comment on how fast they are growing up.

I joined several twin groups on Facebook to get advice and guidance from other parents, and this was huge support for me. I could ask questions and get great advice whenever I needed it. One of the twin groups I was in was a charity called TAMBA (Twin and Multiple Birth Association). I got to join a single-parent group of theirs that was even more useful to me. Through that group, I was put in touch with another new Mum who had also lost her husband to cancer and was raising her twins alone. Rachel lived in another part of the country, and we soon became good friends. We'd chat for hours every night when our twins were in bed. We'd talk about our husbands and the heartache we'd been through and were still going through. We gave each other encouragement that we could do this on our own. We'd share tips for making things easier for ourselves. As the years went by, we stayed in touch. We'd only ever talked via messages, but it felt like we'd known each other for years. We would share in each other's accomplishments and happiness and watch our twins grow up. We never thought we'd ever meet in person living so far apart. To our amazement, we actually got to meet for the first time this year thanks to some mutual friends. It was amazing to finally see in person the lady who'd helped me through so many dark times, but also see how happy she was now and finally meet her boys.

Over the years, there have been so many funny incidents when I have been out with them. I've been asked how I tell them apart even when Archie has been dressed in blue and Ella in pink. One time I couldn't stop myself and stated, "he has a penis, and she has a vagina." I have never seen the colour of someone's face change so quickly. They ran off with a very red face, and that has to be my favourite response to all the crazy questions. I was also once asked, "are they twins? How did that happen?". I was so tempted to explain how babies are made, but instead, I politely said, "I got lucky". With twins, you're guaranteed to get the typical 'double trouble', it does get frustrating, but then you remember it's double the love too.

When Emma and I would take them out together, people often thought we were a couple, and we never bothered to correct them, we'd just link arms, smile, and go along with it. We used to laugh at how often this would happen.

There were times when I was out on my own with them, and people would ask if my husband helped with the night feeds or did we take turns. I'd just smile and say yes, he helps, but in my head, I'd be screaming I wish he was here to help, but he's dead. Those moments were the reality check that I was all they had, and I was a single Mum to twins.

When they were around eighteen months, I decided to start them at nursery, I needed time for myself, and they needed to learn to socialise without me constantly being with them. This was the best decision for all of us. Just being able to go food shopping, go and get my nails done, or pop and see a friend meant so much to me. They stayed at nursery until they started school. By then, they were ready for the school environment, and they were bright children and eager to learn.

I decided to take them to America when they were twenty months old. I was desperate to see my brother and his family again, so I thought, why not. People thought I was crazy for doing a long-haul flight with two toddlers, but I didn't care. I was determined to do this for all of us. Amazingly they coped fantastically on the flights there and back. The cabin crew was lovely watching the twins when I needed the toilet and checking if I needed any help. They even commented on what lovely children they were and how settled they'd been. We even received help from the captain of one of the flights to help us get to our connecting flight. I was doing all this with a double pushchair, two car seats, and hand luggage. Anyone seeing us must've thought I was insane! But I did it. I managed to take my children on their first holiday. We spent three weeks in America. Unfortunately, the first week they were both really ill with chest infections, and seeking medical help was not easy, but once they were started on antibiotics and started improving, our holiday really started. I took them to the local park to play when Paul and his family were at work and school. Once they broke up for Christmas, we were really able to start enjoying ourselves. We had trips out and spent time together, and I even managed a trip to the nail salon whilst Paul looked after the twins. It was fantastic. I loved sharing Christmas with them and having someone else help show the twins the magic of Christmas. My favourite part of the trip was our visit to Disneyland. The whole day was amazing, and watching the night-time parade and fireworks was magical. They met Mickey Mouse but weren't too sure about him. They went on some of the little rides and saw lots of the various characters there. They don't really remember the trip, but at least I have that memory, and so does my brother.

When the twins were two, I decided it was time for us to get a dog. I'd grown up with dogs and wanted my children to too. They were nervous around dogs. I wanted them not to fear them but also learn to respect them and get the love and affection I knew dogs could give. I knew I wanted a Labrador. I knew the temperament was great with children. I also wanted a dog for protection, safety, and companionship. I knew I'd get that with a Labrador, so I started looking. I stumbled across a litter of black Labradors not too far away. I went to visit on my own. I instantly fell in love. There were only two left. I'd have taken them both, but I knew one dog would be enough for us. So a few weeks later, Albie joined our family, he settled straight in, and he and the twins became inseparable. They formed a bond I knew couldn't be broken, Albie loved his kids, and they loved him.

The day they started school, they were excited but scared. Luckily a few of the children that went to their nursery were also going to their school. They thrived from day one at school. They are extremely bright children and are like little sponges. They're eager to learn and enjoy the activities and learning they do at school. They have been fortunate enough to have had lovely teachers throughout their time there.

As the years have gone by, I have watched Archie and Ella develop their own little personalities and characters. Archie is the outgoing one who likes to make everyone laugh, the class clown. His energy levels are off the chart, he never stops running around, and he never stops talking either. I often ask him where his off switch is, and he just laughs at me. He was born to be on stage. He's always singing and dancing around. He's a very affectionate boy and tells me he'll look after me when he's a man, and he'll do all the jobs around the house. He loves his Mum!

Ella is so different from Archie. She can be very quiet but inside, her mind is always on the go. She is extremely affectionate and loves cuddling the people she loves. She is so creative and very arty. She loves to read and draw pictures. She has no fear when it comes to climbing and trying new activities. Her strength amazes me, and along with her intelligence, I see a lot of my Mum in her. If she puts her mind down to it, she can do anything.

Both my children, I truly believe, will go far in life. They are both academic and already know things I have no idea about.

They play together most of the time but do fight a lot. I've lost count of the amount of times I've had to separate them for fighting and hurting each other or arguing. But when I witness the moments where they're walking along hand in hand, giving each other a hug, or helping each other, my heart melts. They may drive me insane most days, but deep down, I know they are great kids. They are polite, well-behaved most of the time, and very caring.

The bond between them is incredible to watch, they've always played together, but there's more to their relationship than two children playing. They always have to be with each other, and they'll sit next to each other when they're reading or playing on their electronics. If I separate them from arguing, they'll sit in their rooms so they can see each other across the hall while they play on their own. Ella does mother Archie a lot and will do things for him even though he's perfectly capable. I really hope they keep the strong bond as they continue to grow up. I think they will always look out for each other and protect each other as they already do this.

I have always encouraged my children to be active, and along with dog walking, I enrolled them in MMA. I felt not only was it important they know how to protect and defend themselves but also, karate is in their blood. It was a natural move for them. They have now been doing mixed martial arts for five years. They have worked their way up the belts and are currently training for their brown belt, which they hope to achieve next year.

Along with karate, I also enrolled them in swimming lessons as I am a weak swimmer, and I did not want them to be like me. They've now been swimming for six years and are about to complete stage six. They are great little swimmers. It reassures me they will know what to do if ever faced with a dangerous situation.

As a parent, all I want to do is protect my children. However, I know that isn't always possible, and they must learn their own lessons through experiences. I don't push any of my beliefs onto Archie and Ella and encourage them to form their own opinions and beliefs. They have the right to choose their own path. I'm here to guide them the best I can. I watch my children grow every day, amazed by the strength and determination they show for life. They know who they are and aren't afraid to show this. They are so much more confident than I ever was at their age.

They have learnt some hard lessons very early in life, it breaks my heart they had to learn about loss at such a young age, but I was determined they would know everything about their Dad, who he was, the kind of man he was and his dreams for them, Over the years we have laughed and cried at the stories I have told them. I made them both memory books that contain messages and comments from Facebook about John from the moment I posted the announcement of his death and the years that followed. By having this book, they are able to see what John truly meant to all the people whose lives he touched. I also made them a photo book of his life from birth through to our last holiday together. Having these has enabled them to feel closer to him and learn about him. Whenever they want to feel close to their Dad, they sit and read their books and cuddle their 'Daddy bear.' I bought them both a special bear that they call 'Daddy Bear.' Whenever they miss their Dad, they cuddle their bear and imagine the cuddles are with John. It's heart-breaking watching your children cry for their father, the man they never met but they love so much. They know he lives on through them, and I often remind them what qualities of his they inherited every time they smile and are comforted.

When the twins were 4 years old, we entered a race with St Teresa's Hospice. The hospice supported both John and me throughout his illness and after he passed away. I asked Archie and Ella if they wanted to do the race for their dad and raise some money to help them as they had helped us. They jumped at the chance, and it was a 5k race around a park in town. They took their sponsor sheets to school and around the neighbourhood, telling people what they were doing and why. They raised nearly £500m they were so proud. We did the race on a nice sunny day, and some friends joined us too. When we had collected all the sponsorship money, we took it to the hospice, who were so happy and moved by Archie and Ella and their story. They asked if they'd be interested in getting their photo taken, holding a big cheque, and being interviewed by the local paper. They thought this was fantastic, and they were little celebrities. They answered questions about John and did a great interview. The article went in the paper, and their little faces lit up when they saw their picture in the paper.

I am beyond proud of the strength they have shown and continue to show. Nothing holds them back. Whatever path they choose for the future, I will be there every step of the way, cheering them on.

Chapter Thirteen – Quality of Life

You never realise how important your senses are until one of them changes. Sight, smell, taste, touch, and sound are there, helping to make sense of everyday life. Lose one, and your whole world is turned upside down.

As I'd focused on the twins for the last few months, the issue of my hearing loss had been pushed to one side. Now they were here, and I was starting to realise how much being partially deaf was impacting my life. I couldn't cope with being in noisy environments, and it was so overwhelming. I didn't know what direction the noises were coming from and certainly couldn't hold a conversation. I was struggling to hear the twins at times, and this caused a lot of anxiety as I was worried I wouldn't be able to hear them cry when they needed me. On top of that, my balance had been impacted, It wasn't too bad when I was standing still. But walking in a straight line was extremely difficult. It was a similar feeling to when you've had too much alcohol, and you just can't quite focus on where your next step needs to go. I found if I had something to hold on to, my balance was greatly improved, and pushing the twins' pram helped immensely with that. As I adjusted to the change in sound, my ability to balance improved, it took several years but at least now I can walk without looking intoxicated.

I had to do something about my hearing as it was hugely impacting my life. I arranged an appointment at the hospital to discuss my options. They did a full hearing test and confirmed I had completely lost my hearing in my left ear, but thankfully, my right ear had normal hearing levels. My best option was to be fitted with a cross-aid hearing aid. This would create the effect of hearing in both ears and enable me to program it to focus on voices.

When I was fitted with my cross aid, the difference was amazing, and I could hear sounds I hadn't heard for a while. But the best sound was my babies, and I could hear every little noise they made. Tears of joy rolled down my face as I was given the ability to hear again. Ok, it wasn't the same as having my full hearing back, but it was definitely an improvement.

It gave me a whole new appreciation of the world, being outside was so different. I could hear the wind blowing, leaves rustling, and birds singing. I know it sounds corny, but it was such a beautiful experience.

My confidence was starting to grow again now I could function better. I was able to go out more again, I started taking the twins to playgroups and was able to hold a conversation. I'd learned to lip-read a bit since losing my hearing, so I still relied on this when places were a little louder than I could cope with.

I still struggled in places with loud music on or lots of people talking at the same time. I wasn't able to zone into the person I was having a conversation with. The noises came from all directions. I was unable to work out the direction sounds were coming from. As the twins were getting more active, they needed to go to new places like soft play. The soft play was a form of hell for me, especially when the twins were running around and didn't need me constantly by their side. The volume of noise in soft play is horrific, with constant screaming coming from all directions. With screaming being so high pitched, it caused further issues for me as the sound going through my cross-aid caused pain in my ears. I was also struggling with the fact I couldn't focus on my own children's voices. I was unable to take them to soft play on my own for fear of not being able to hear them and make sure they were safe.

The cross-aid had helped me so much, but it wasn't enough, and I needed something better. I was told of a specialist hearing shop that may be able to help me, so I made an appointment. Off I went and explained my situation and why I was struggling with the cross-aid the hospital had given me. Another full hearing assessment was completed, and recommendations were made on the types of hearing aids that would help me. After a lot of deliberation, I picked a top-of-the-range cross-aid. Their technology was so advanced compared to the hospitals. My new cross-aid was ordered, and when it finally came and was fitted, I was amazed at how tiny and discreet it was. It even blended in with my hair colour, and I was so excited to see how different it was.

What a difference an upgrade in technology made. I could hear in even more detail, I was amazed when I first got my original cross-aid, but this was a whole other level. The detail I could hear was astonishing, I had finally found the right device for me, and for the price of it, I was expecting something special, and that's exactly what I got. It should hopefully last me around ten years before I need to upgrade it unless technology advances to the point something new is invented, or they can restore my hearing. Now that would be amazing!

Don't get me wrong, it hasn't given me the full experience of getting my hearing back, but it's certainly got me a lot closer. It's frustrating if my batteries run out while I'm away from home, having to change the batteries every 3 days, keep it clean, and have annual check-ups to ensure it is still doing its job. But if doing all this is the price to pay to have a better quality of life, then it's worth it. This is the hand I have been dealt, it is my choice how I manage it, and the only person responsible for doing everything possible to give me the life I want is me.

Chapter Fourteen - Shave It

I knew after losing John I wanted to do something for charity and raise awareness of brain tumours, but I didn't know what. Then one day, I saw the 'Shave It' campaign for Macmillan Cancer. People voluntarily shaved their hair off to raise money for charity, and it planted a seed in my head. I thought long and hard about it, I didn't want to lose my hair, but neither did my Mum or John. Cancer took that choice away from them as it does for so many people. By having my hair shaved off, it would enable me to understand more about the journey both John and my Mum went through. That was it my decision was made. As always, I spoke to Emma about my plan, and she had her doubts. She'd seen how much I had struggled with my appearance since my operation and was concerned with the mental and emotional effect this would have on me. She was always completely honest with me, which is one of the many reasons I turn to her whenever I need advice. But as always, Emma made it clear she would support me whatever decision I made, and she knew I'd do it, every time I got an idea in my head, I normally jumped straight in.

I set up my just-giving page, giving a brief overview of the story of John and my Mum and my reasons for doing the campaign. I wanted to give something back to the people who had been there for John and me and also raise awareness. Immediately the sponsors started coming in, and people were happy to support my quest to raise as much money as I could.

I set a target of £500. I thought surely that would be achievable.

I decided the day for shaving my hair would be the 23rd of July, John's birthday. It felt like the perfect day, as seen as he was my inspiration for doing this. I'd already arranged with my hairdresser Paul to do the shave, so it was done properly. Paul generously offered a free gift voucher to raffle off for a free colour, cut, and blow dry. This created a lot of extra sponsors. The raffle would be drawn on the day of the shave.

We even decided to invite the local paper to help raise awareness. As you can imagine, the local paper jumped at the chance for a story, and I did not envision what would follow.

The day of the shave arrived, I was nervous but also excited. I was doing something positive to help make a difference, and only good could come out of this. I got to the salon, and the reporter and photographer arrived too. We had a little chat about how we would do this, and they decided they would video the shave so that it could go live on their website with the story. Why not, I thought, it's for a good cause. The shave was nerve-racking, but Paul was so good at keeping my spirits up and made me enjoy the whole experience. The end look was very dramatic compared to my long blonde hair, but I also felt empowered by what I had done. I was making a difference, something positive was coming out of all this heartache, and that was much-needed money for a charity that helps so many families every day.

The next day my story was in the paper. I thought it would be a short article in the middle of the paper. How wrong I was, I was on the front page! A picture of the twins and me took up half the page, and the story was on the front cover and inside. I did not expect this. The next thing I knew, people were knocking on my front door, wanting my story and wanting to write articles about me. What the hell was happening? I was just an ordinary woman raising money for charity.

I walked to my local supermarket and was followed there by a journalist hounding me for my story, even offering me money to take my photo. It was absolute madness. Walking around the supermarket people were looking at me and looking at the newspaper, they realised it was me. Standing in the queue, I could see more people turning and looking at me. This wasn't what I'd wanted to happen, but it was too late now.

The knocks at the door continued for several days, and I ended up having to get an agency to represent me to stop everyone hounding me. My story was going national, and there was nothing I could do about it, instead, I just had to jump on board and make sure it was told in the best possible way.

A few days later, my story reached even more people across the country, and it was moving people to tears with sadness but also giving hope through the beauty of my miracle twins. More and more people would turn to look at me when I was out. This took some getting used to, especially with me still lacking confidence in the way I looked because of the paralysis.

Next came the offer of magazine deals. I initially said no, but as time went on and the continuous bombardment of offers came, I finally gave in. I made it clear I didn't want just any old magazine, nothing cheap and tacky. I want a good quality magazine with the right target audience. This wasn't about making money, this was about raising awareness. In the end, I signed a deal with

‘Women’s Own’. Yet again, my story went to print and out to the country. Between the newspapers and the magazine, my story was out there for everyone to read. As with all articles, they are never 100% accurate, and parts of the story weren’t right, but at least I was getting my message out there and was raising awareness, I was proud of that. I’d achieved what I’d set out to do, and I’d raised just over £1250, more than doubled my original target. When I think back to that time, it was insane, a complete whirlwind it had been. I remember being happy to go back to getting on with my life.

Chapter Fifteen - Another Shock

After my brain surgery, I knew I would need regular scans to monitor whether it would return, especially with 5% of it being left. When I went for my first consultation with my Neurosurgeon a few months after my surgery, I was not prepared for what I was going to find out.

My Neurosurgeon advised that he was happy with how the surgery went and that I appeared to be coping well. He advised that my paralysis would improve with time, exercise, and patience, although I would never make a full recovery. The thought of never getting my old face back hit me hard. I wanted to be myself again and felt like a big part of me was missing as I didn't look like myself anymore. This made me determined to be the first person to make a full recovery and gave me the fight I needed.

However, I was not prepared for the answer to one question that had been foremost in my head. 'If my tumour started growing, would the change be quick?' My Neurosurgeon went on to explain it was a slow-growing tumour, and looking back to my scan five years early. It had grown from 4mm to 4cm. Did I just hear him right? All I could stutter out was, 'excuse me, what scan showed my tumour?'. I had had an MRI scan done in 2008 as I had presented with tremors and my GP at the time wanted to find out the cause. I was told the scan showed nothing of concern. However, my Neurosurgeon didn't agree. He stated it clearly showed a 4mm tumour that had not been included in the report. 'Wow, are you kidding me!' I thought. I, therefore, asked what would have been done if the tumour had been identified five years ago. He advised I would have been referred to himself. He would've arranged Stereotactic Radiotherapy that would have killed the tumour. I wouldn't have lost my hearing, and I wouldn't have been left with paralysis. I would have been me and had regular check-ups and scans to ensure it didn't regrow. At this point, I broke down in tears. I couldn't believe that my life could have been so different if only they had seen my tumour. I knew I couldn't let this go and would do a lot of thinking following my appointment.

I spent a few days processing this information, and I then made the decision to seek legal advice. I contacted a Solicitor that specialised in medical negligence. Their advice was to initially write a letter to the hospital stating what I had found out and ask for an investigation. Once I received a response, I then needed to contact the Solicitor to start legal proceedings.

Writing the letter and waiting for a response took several months. I felt like I was being ignored, and I was getting more frustrated as time went on. I had been robbed of my hearing and face unnecessarily. To say I was fuming is an understatement. Eventually, I received my response, an apology. That was it. Are you serious? Did they seriously think that was acceptable? This drove me to take this further. Legal proceedings were initiated.

The whole process of putting together a case to finally get an outcome took six years. The process was handled excellently by my Solicitor and Barrister. It was very emotional at times, giving my statement. I had to go to several appointments in Newcastle with my Solicitor and go to Sheffield to be examined by a different Neurologist who was one of my expert witnesses. He was a lovely man. He put me through numerous tests so that he could make an informed decision on my condition and prognosis. Again I cried during this examination, I was reliving everything all over again. This happened numerous times throughout the case. As further evidence was gained, they needed to obtain the full facts about how my life had been affected, my health, and my ability to work and care for my children.

Emma was interviewed as a witness for me. She was able to advise how my tumour had affected me, the changes she had seen in my personality, and the care I had needed from my friends and family.

An independent Radiographer was also consulted to gain an opinion on whether he thought the tumour should have been identified back in 2008. He confirmed it should have been.

All evidence was on my side, and the opposition was given time to build their case before meetings started taking place between my Solicitor and the defendant's Solicitor. It was a long, drawn-out process, and they denied medical negligence, which meant the case would have to go to court. The thought of having to take the stand and tell my story in front of strangers scared me greatly, but it was the principle that this shouldn't have happened that kept me going, and I certainly didn't want it happening to anyone else. So we prepared our case for court.

The court date was set, all statements were ready, and we knew my case was strong and were ready to fight to win this case. Then the settlement offers started coming in. We had already worked out the value of my case. I'd have a comfortable life if I got the full value, but no amount of money would give me back what I had lost, my hearing, my face, my smile, photos with my children, my job prospects, and my social life. How can you put a price on that? The mental damage it had done to me was unreal. I'd always thought I was a strong person up to this point. Thankfully working with a Neuropsychologist got me back on track and focused. I was ready for court, and I was ready to fight for my case.

The offers of settlement, to begin with, were ridiculous. Were they for real? How insulting, I thought. Obviously, they were refused, but after a few offers and negotiations, a figure was finally agreed upon. It wouldn't give me my life back, only I could do that, but it would help me provide for my children and give them a good future, so I accepted their offer. It took several months from agreeing on a settlement figure to actually get the money, but I'd waited six years. What difference would a few months make?

Finally, I received the call to confirm my Solicitor had received the money. A few days later, it was in my account. I could put it to good use and move on with my life.

I'd been through so much, more than I ever dreamt I would, yes, I could've kept pushing and gone to court, but I was emotionally and mentally drained. I knew money wasn't the answer to this fight. What I wanted was to be acknowledged, have someone take responsibility, and say sorry, this shouldn't have happened to you. I never got the apology. Would it have even made a difference? Probably not. One thing I do know is it has made me even stronger, and I'm not afraid to stand up for what I believe in. I have come close to the breaking point so many times since I lost John, but I've always managed to rise back up and face everything thrown my way and will continue to do so.

Chapter Sixteen - More Treatment

Throughout my recovery, I have followed every bit of advice I have been given. I have worked with a physiotherapist, an eye consultant, a hearing consultant, my Neurosurgeon, a Radiographer, and a Neuropsychologist. I have been hooked up to machines, had a painful procedure on my eye, regular eye check-ups, hearing tests, fitted with hearing aids, and more. All of this I have done to aid my recovery. Out of all of these, the hardest by far was having

Stereotactic Radiotherapy. This is basically gamma rays going straight into your brain. I went to Sheffield in 2014 for the procedure, and it was agreed I would undergo the procedure to kill the remaining tumour to prevent further growth.

Off I went with Emma by my side yet again, not knowing what to expect and hoping it would work. The procedure involved having a cage screwed to the outside of my head. This was done with a local anaesthetic, and four screws were literally screwed into my skull. I could feel every screw go in, but it didn't hurt. I could hear the noise of them forcing the screws into my head. I just took it all in my stride, and the nursing staff were surprised they'd seen grown men break down in tears having the cage attached to their head. I wasn't bothered, although I did want a photo to remind me, Emma took a photo of me with my cage, a big grin on my face, and gave the thumbs up to show I was ok. The purpose of the cage was so that my head was kept perfectly still whilst the gamma rays were sent directly to my tumour and didn't hit any other brain tissue. I was laid on a table and pushed into a machine very similar to an MRI machine. I laid in there for around 40 minutes whilst they zapped my brain. They played music to help me relax. To be honest, I was very comfortable and came close to falling asleep. I had spent the best part of the day with the cage on my head. My neck was tired from the weight of it. Laying down was a relief. Once the treatment was over, I had to spend a few hours in the ward to ensure I was ok before they could discharge me.

Emma drove me home that evening. I was exhausted and just wanted my bed.

Whilst I'd been away, John's Mum had stayed at my house and looked after the twins. I had missed them so much and couldn't wait to see their little faces again. I had never been separated from them, but this treatment was essential to help my recovery.

It took a few weeks for the holes in my head to heal, but thankfully they didn't leave any lasting scars. After that, I had scans yearly to check if there was any growth and see how I was recovering. After surgery, my paralysis was classed as grade 4, which is the most severe. As time went on, I made improvements and am now a grade 2. There is still time for me to make a full recovery. Hopefully, I will. I get times when the sensation in my face changes or it starts twitching, and I'm always hopeful when this happens as it's possibly a sign the nerves are waking up a bit more. I occasionally get synkinesis, which is unwanted contractions of the muscles in my face when I move a different area of my face. This tends to happen when I close my eye, and it can cause the corner of my mouth to move. I have no control over this movement, and it is definitely a strange session. When this happens, I have to focus really hard to try and stop the involuntary movement and only move the part of my face I want to. It can be embarrassing at times, but the only thing I can do is keep practicing my exercises and focus. One day it may stop happening, who knows?

Chapter Seventeen - Getting on with Life

As the twins were getting closer to starting school, I decided it was time to get back into the world of working again. I had been a full-time Mum since they were born but knew the time was right to go back to work, have adult contact and start providing for my family.

I knew I couldn't return to my previous job of being a Tutor due to my hearing loss. I couldn't cope with noisy environments as I couldn't hear people talking to me. I needed to find a job that could utilise the skill set I had and be flexible enough to work around the kids' school hours.

I was very lucky to be invited to an interview for the first job I applied for. It was for an Administrative Assistant in my local council, I had never done an admin role before but hoped my management experience and requirements for a job of this nature would be enough for me to be a suitable candidate. I was petrified when I went to the interview, I'd always enjoyed interviews in the past, but this time I was very self-conscious and thought the fact I hadn't worked for the last four years didn't go against me.

I turned up for my interview thinking, just be yourself and do your best. It was a panel interview with the Manager of the department, the Duty Manager, and the lady who had been doing the work I would be doing. I answered all the questions they posed to me and explained why I wanted the job and how I thought it would fit my lifestyle and commitments to my family. It was only 15 hours a week which would suit me as long as I could work the hours whilst the twins were at nursery/school.

I couldn't believe it when I received a call the next day offering me the job. I was over the moon. I'd got another part of my life back. I couldn't wait to start! I started work on the 4th of February, 2017. This was a huge turning point in my life. I was becoming more sociable again, using my brain, earning money, and generally enjoying life. Once the twins started school, it became easier to go to work. I was very fortunate to have Managers who were so supportive and flexible when I worked. I'd landed the perfect job, it was a new role that had been created, and I was able to give my input on how it could be developed going forward. I enjoyed my time at work, working with a fantastic group of people and providing for my family.

Now I had one aspect of my life in order. It was time to focus on other areas. Once the twins started school, I became friends with some of the school Mums. Amazingly, there were 3 sets of twins in their school year, a set of boys, a set of girls, and my two. I became good friends with these ladies, one I'd already met through Emma, and Claire had twin girls and an older daughter. Then there was Lindsay with twin boys, and I knew her husband from my school days. And Stacey was the final member of our close group. She had three boys, one being in the same school year as all the twins. As our playground conversation grew, we decided to start going out to our local pub every two weeks. This was fantastic for me. I finally had a social life again and had some more amazing friends. We all supported and confided in each other. I couldn't ask for a better group of friends. We still have our Thursday drinking sessions and meet up with all our children in the school holidays.

So I now had two parts of my life in order, and I felt I was now ready to consider dating again. Well, my eyes were well and truly opened during the couple of years I tried online dating. Between receiving messages that can only be described as pure filth, offers of things that made me blush, attracting men either old enough to be my father or young enough to be my son! This was an experience unlike no other. Chatting to men via messages, I was entering a dating world, unlike the one I'd been in a decade earlier. It was no longer a case of meeting someone when you were on a night out, not when you were nearly forty, that's for sure. Some men came across really nicely until they thought it was ok to talk about sex and ask totally inappropriate questions to someone they had never met. I just couldn't understand why men thought it was ok to act like that!

I did go on a few dates with some nice men, but there was never a spark for either myself or the person I met. I gave up at times and took a few months' break, and then returned to trying again. One guy I dated for a few weeks was lovely and so kind, but he just wasn't right for me. I couldn't explain what it was. I just knew something felt wrong. So again, I gave up for a few months, then tried again, and had another couple of dates, but again no spark, so I decided that was it. I was no longer prepared to keep doing this. If I was meant to meet someone, they would come along when I least expected it.

I carried on focussing on my family. Unfortunately, my beautiful boy Albie has been having some health problems. The poor boy hadn't had the best of luck throughout his life. Double elbow dysplasia at eighteen months old, resulting in a double elbow operation. This was followed by unexplained vomiting the following year, then two cancerous lumps that were removed. After that, he was well for a year but then started developing behavioural problems. He was starting to dominate me, and after consulting with a behaviourist, I learnt he was trying to be the alpha of the family, we worked on this, and he improved. He then had a couple of seizures, so the vets wanted a brain scan in case he had a brain tumour.

My first thought was, you've got to be kidding me. This can't happen again. Thankfully the brain scans showed there was nothing to be concerned about; he probably had epilepsy and was put on medication. He picked up once he was on the medication.

I felt he might benefit from having a playmate as he was so happy when he was with other dogs. I started looking for Labradors for sale. Then I found a litter for sale not too far away from us. I set up a meeting and instantly fell in love with the litter. When the kids and I went to meet the puppies, they still had their eyes closed and weren't even walking. Archie and Ella sat in the pen with the dogs, and one dog started crawling its way to Ella, the breeder moved the dog, and to our surprise, it happened again. The dog had picked Ella. We'd found our newest family member, Archie, named him

Cole. We visited every week until he was ready to come home.

When Albie met Cole, he wasn't sure about him, but he soon grew to love him, and Cole followed him everywhere. They would curl up together whenever they wanted to chill out or sleep, Albie tended to use Cole as a pillow, but Cole didn't care, he loved his big brother. They would charge around the house, pouncing at each other, they were so much fun to watch. Our house was crazy, but it was definitely a happy one. Albie's dominance settled down, and our little family was all happy.

Chapter Eighteen - My Second First

A few days after I'd deleted my dating profiles and the apps I'd been on, to my surprise, I received a message on Instagram from a man I used to go to school with. I thought it was very out of the blue, but I thought it would be nice to catch up, so I replied. We started chatting, and we talked about what had happened in our lives and our children. We were getting on really well. He asked if I wanted to go out for a meal. I thought, 'Why not? It would be nice to go out.' So we arranged to go out on a Saturday. He offered to pick me up as he remembered where I lived when we were kids, as I'd told him I was back in my childhood home, I said yes. Andy told me he drove an old transit van, so he would pick me up in that. I thought, 'oh god, I'm going in a dirty work van'. Thankfully he'd been winding me up and turned up in a car on the Saturday evening. The twins knew I was going out with a man, so they ran to the window to see who I was going out with, and they sat on the window sill with big smiles on their faces waving and watching me leave. I was so embarrassed. I walked out of the house, took one look, and thought, 'Hmm, he looks nice!'. He opened the car door for me, a gentleman from the start. That's a good sign!

We went for a meal in town and talked nonstop. We decided after our meal that we'd go and drop his car at home, as he lived close to me, and walk to our local pub. We carried on talking all night about our school days, our lives, our children, and our jobs. I felt a definite spark. The night went by so quickly I didn't want it to end, but it was closing time, and I had to get home to the babysitter. He walked me home. He was holding my hand all the way home. It felt so natural. When we reached my house, I was gutted the night was over, he kissed me, and wow, there was that spark. If I was chocolate, I would've melted it. I hadn't felt like that in years. We said our goodbyes, and off he went home. My babysitter took one look at me and knew I'd had a good night. He texted me when he got home, thanking me for a lovely night, and told me he'd like to see me again. 'Hell yeah,' I thought but didn't want to come across too strongly, so I said yes, that would be nice.

The next morning he texted me. He told me his Mum had said she could tell he'd had a good night as she hadn't seen him smile like that in a long time. I wanted to see him so badly. As it turned out that morning, as me and the kids were walking home with our dogs, we bumped into one of their school friends who asked if they wanted to go to their house to play. Her Mum said, yes, I could have a few hours to myself. I jumped at the chance. I texted Andy, saying I was child-free for a few hours. He suggested I go round to his house. I'd told him about a fault on one of the seat belts in my car. He'd said he'd take a look at it for me, so this gave us both a perfect reason for me to go around.

Off I went. He fixed my car quickly, so we decided to go for a walk. Again we talked constantly. It was so easy and felt so natural. He gave me another kiss before I left. There was that spark again. We'd talked about how often we'd be able to see each other. We had two options, either go out every couple of weeks when I could get a babysitter, or he could come round to my house once the twins were in bed. We decided he'd come to my house that night. My dogs went crazy when he came in, they loved him instantly, and he loved them. We had another lovely night. We both agreed we didn't want to rush into anything, and we'd let nature take its course.

Well, nature worked very quickly as he started coming around every night, bringing treats for the dogs every time. Obviously, they loved his nightly visits. We talked about anything and everything and obviously had a few kisses. It became our routine. The twins knew I'd started seeing someone, but I wasn't ready for them to meet him yet. I told them I needed time to get to know him before they would meet him. As it turned out, a month after we started dating, he met them. We went to Seaton Carew, played on the beach, ate fish and chips, and played in the playground and the arcades. The kids loved it. They went to bed with big grins on their faces that night. Now Andy had met the kids, and he was able to come around earlier. He started having tea with us most nights, and the kids were constantly asking when Andy was coming around. They'd definitely accepted him. He showed an interest in them, talked to them, and played with them. He'd certainly won them over. It made me so happy watching the three of them together. I knew there was potential in this relationship.

As time went on, we spent more and more time together. The twins went for a sleepover for a few days, so we took this opportunity to spend more time together and decided to have a day trip to York one day. We had a fantastic time, drinking, eating, and enjoying each other's company. We grew closer over those few days and talked about having a future together. We both wanted the same thing. To be happy and be with someone who accepted us for who we were, we'd both found what we were looking for. Andy still spent time with his friends, and I spent time with my friends. All aspects of my life were finally feeling complete again.

We fell in love quickly and talked about how we knew the spark was there from the first night. I never expected any of it, let alone with someone I knew from my childhood. I'd thought I would spend the rest of my life on my own, and now I had a man who loved me, loved my children, and wanted to have a future with me. I felt like the luckiest woman in the world. I had found my second first.

Remember the vision I mentioned previously, the twins, a black Labrador running around a meadow with the tall, dark man in the background. Something tells me that man was Andy.

Andy moved in with us later in the year, we became a family, and he became a father figure to my children. He was so understanding of my situation and how I wanted to keep John's memory alive for my children. He fully supported me with everything. He listened to me talk about him, and he listened to my children talk about their Dad and what he would've been like. This made me love him even more, and he was everything I wanted. The connection we had was amazing, the chemistry was unbelievable, and we fit together perfectly.

We have been together for over three years now, and the twins tell me he's like a Dad to them. They refer to him as their 'Bonus Dad'. I'm finally happy and looking forward to the future.

Chapter Nineteen - Family Life

So family life now consisted of me, Andy, two crazy kids, and two crazy dogs. We were very happy, but then Covid hit and turned the whole world upside down, and we were thrown into lockdown. This was going to be one hell of a test on our newly formed relationship.

During Covid, Albie became very ill. He was getting tired very easily and not eating properly. Something was wrong, but we didn't know what. He needed tests to find out what was going on, but these tests needed to be conducted by a specialist vet. This meant travelling out of the area to one, and I was so grateful when my friend Helen offered to take Albie and me for these tests. Helen and I had become friends a few years earlier when Albie and her black Labrador Jack became the best of friends. We'd done so many walks together with the dogs and the kids we had become very close. Albie adored her, so she was happy to go in the car with her. Unfortunately, Covid had impacted the way vet appointments were conducted, so all I could do was pass my boy over to the vet and wait and see what they found. After numerous tests and visits to the specialist vet, they found his body was not producing enough red blood cells, which was causing his body to shut down. His cancer was back, and it was attacking his whole body. The vet discussed the next step. We could try a blood transfusion, and it may give us a couple more weeks, but even then, Albie's quality of life wouldn't be much better. It would be more for us so we could have more time with him. He'd only just turned five. I couldn't believe what was happening to my beautiful body. We brought him home to think about what we should do. He gradually got slower. We knew it was time. You could see in his eyes he'd had enough. I made the call to the vet and agreed it was time to put him to sleep. Andy and I took Albie on his last car ride, and Helen met us at the vet. She was just as devastated as we were. The vets were fantastic. Even with all the Covid restrictions in place, they made sure we were able to be with our boy when he took his last breath. They took him inside to check him over before bringing him out to us.

They set up a blanket outside the surgery and brought him out. He gave a little wag of his tail when he saw us all and went straight to Andy. Typical, he went to the one that brought him treats! He lay down, and I hugged and kissed him over and over, telling him how sorry I was that I had to let him go. Yet again, I was watching another loved one take their last breath.

Losing Albie caused my depression to surface again, but again I knew the signs, so I contacted my doctor and was prescribed medication to help. Thankfully this time, I had Andy by my side to help keep me strong. Between losing Albie and the restrictions of Covid, I was finding life hard. I'm sure there were millions of people around the world struggling more than I was. We all had to do whatever we could to get through an extremely unsettling time.

When the lockdown finally came to an end, I was thankful for so many things. My children had coped exceptionally well throughout the pandemic, yes, they had had times they were extremely upset and missing their friends and family, but as we were key workers, they were still attending school. I feel this made a huge difference for my two as they had some kind of normality while the rest of the world was stuck at home. Thankfully, my and Andy's relationship had survived lockdown, for a relationship that hadn't even seen its first year when the pandemic hit. I think we were thrown into a huge test on how strong we were as a couple and whether we would pass this test. If anything, I feel it made us stronger, and amazingly, we never once argued.

So life returned to normal for us all. We were back to seeing our friends and family again and living life to the full. The kids were happy, Cole was happy, and we were happy.

Before Covid hit, we had planned our first family holiday to Paris, staying at Eurocamp. We were all so excited to go, but unfortunately, that holiday never happened. Andy and I decided we needed a holiday now all the restrictions had been lifted, but we didn't want to go abroad until life was completely back to normal. We ended up investing in a tent and camping equipment. That summer, we had numerous trips away, each one a new adventure for us all, and most importantly, we were making memories as a family. We will get our holidays abroad in the near future, at least we can say we had a fun-filled summer.

Now life was going so well that the next step was my job. I was ready for a change and wanted to start working full-time. I felt the kids were old enough, and as a family, we would benefit from me working full time. I was over the moon when I landed a new role working with young people supporting them with education and employment. I work from home, so I am there for my children. Cole loves having me home every day with him, and I am doing a job I thoroughly enjoy.

As for the future, who knows what it will bring but I know one thing, whatever is thrown our way, we'll face it together and make the most of every moment.